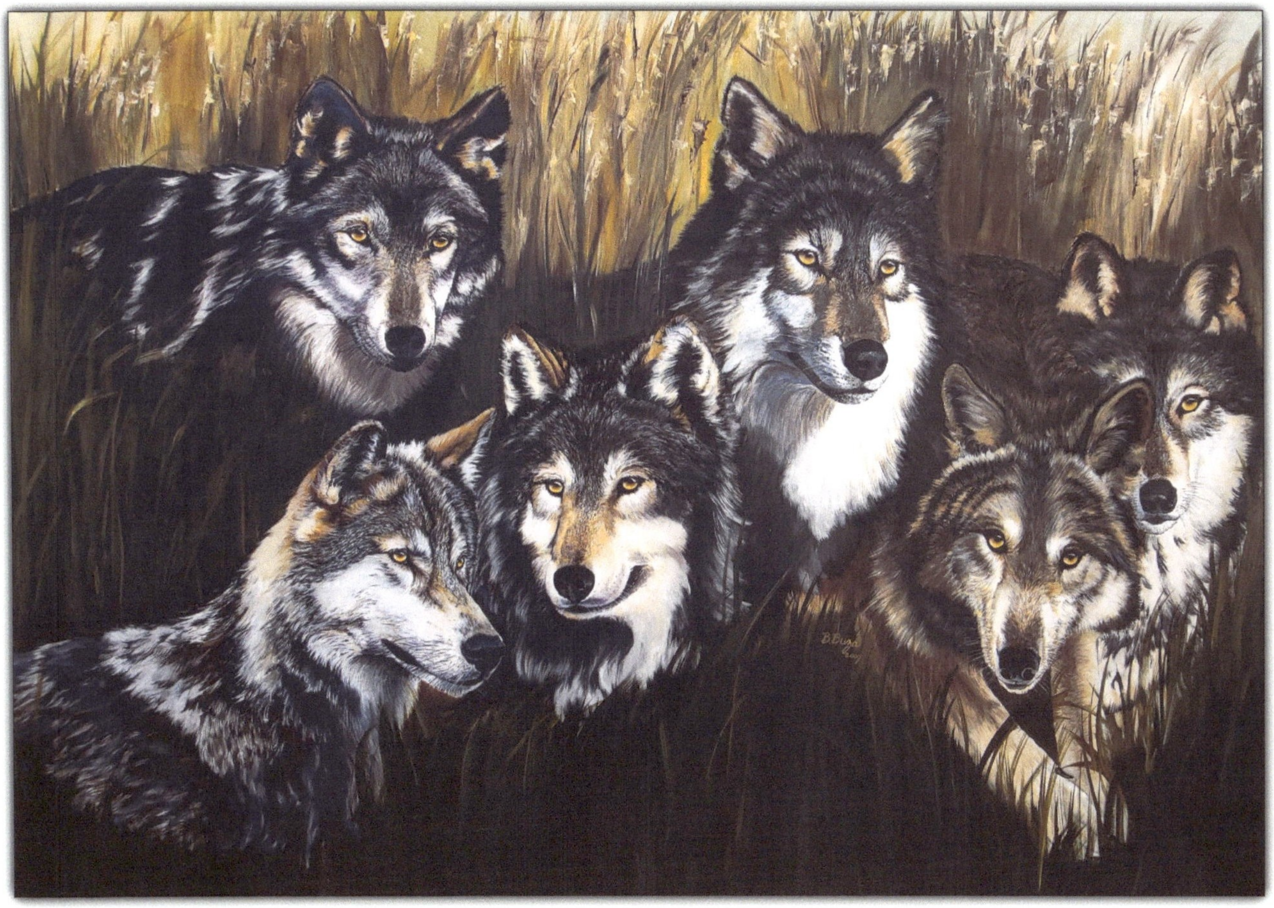

ISBN: 9798868237669 (Paperback)
ISBN: 9798870232539 (Hardcover)

Scripture quotations are taken from the World Edition Bible unless otherwise noted. Published 1997, 2020. Public domain.

Front cover image by Barb Buza.
Book design by Barb Buza.

Printed by Amazon KDP, in the United States of America.
Amazon and the Amazon logo are trademarks of Amazon.com, Inc., or its affiliates.

First printing edition 2023.

Job

Where Were You?

Thrown to the Wolves

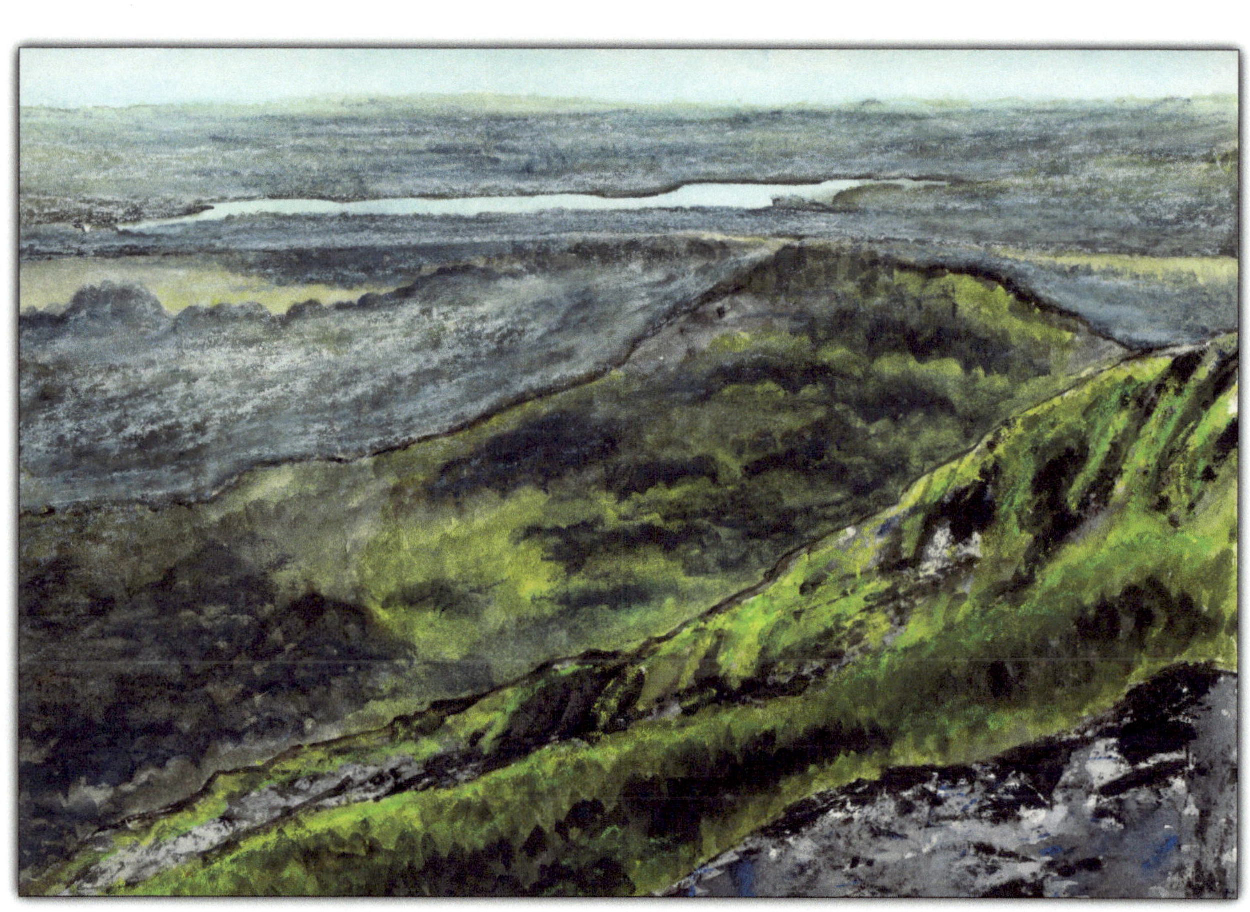

*4 "Where were you when I laid the foundations of the earth?
Declare, if you have understanding.
5 Who determined its measures, if you know?
Or who stretched the line on it?*

Job 38:4-5

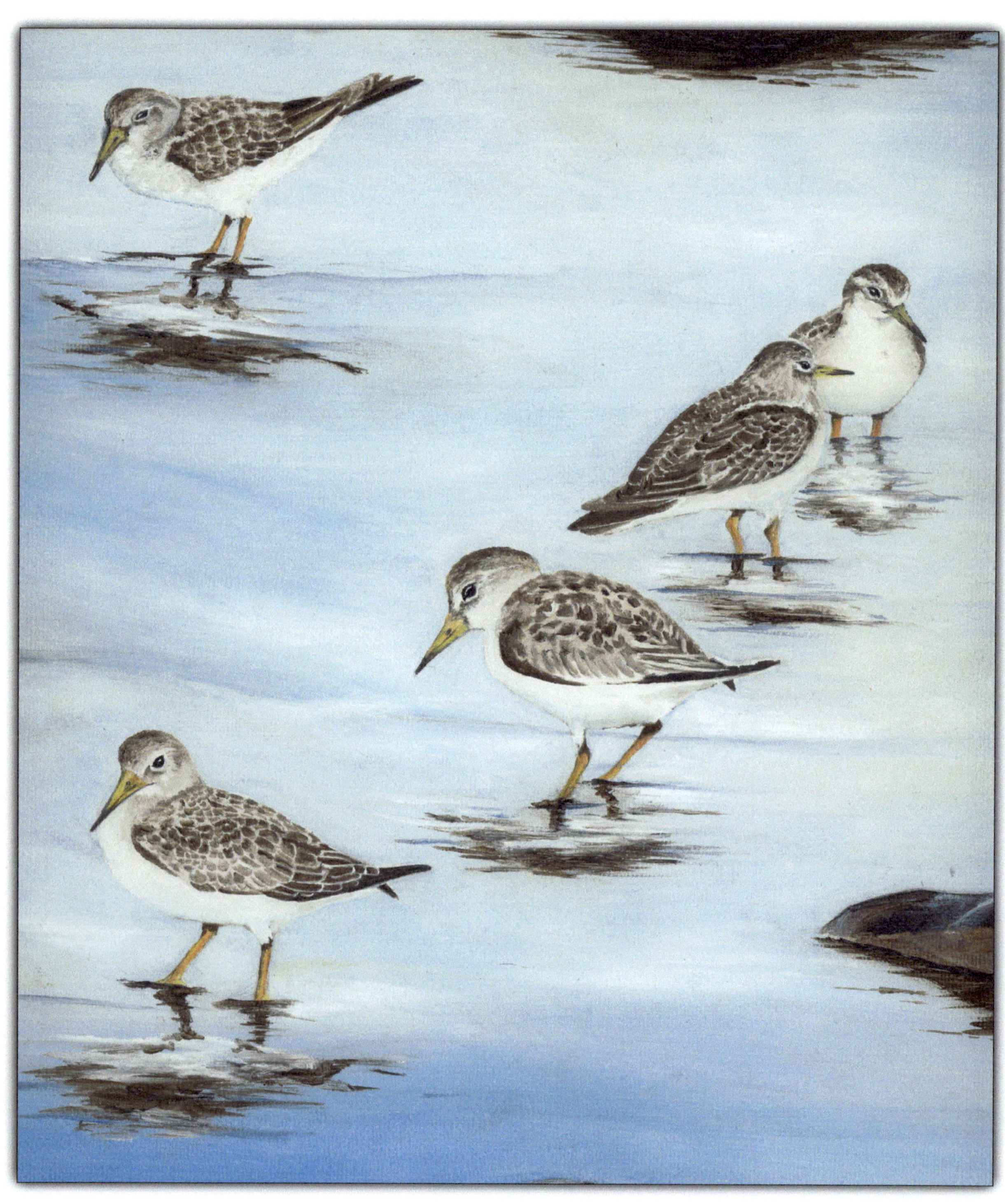

*6 What were its foundations fastened on?
Or who laid its cornerstone,
7 when the morning stars sang together,
and all the sons of God shouted for joy?*

Job 38:6-7

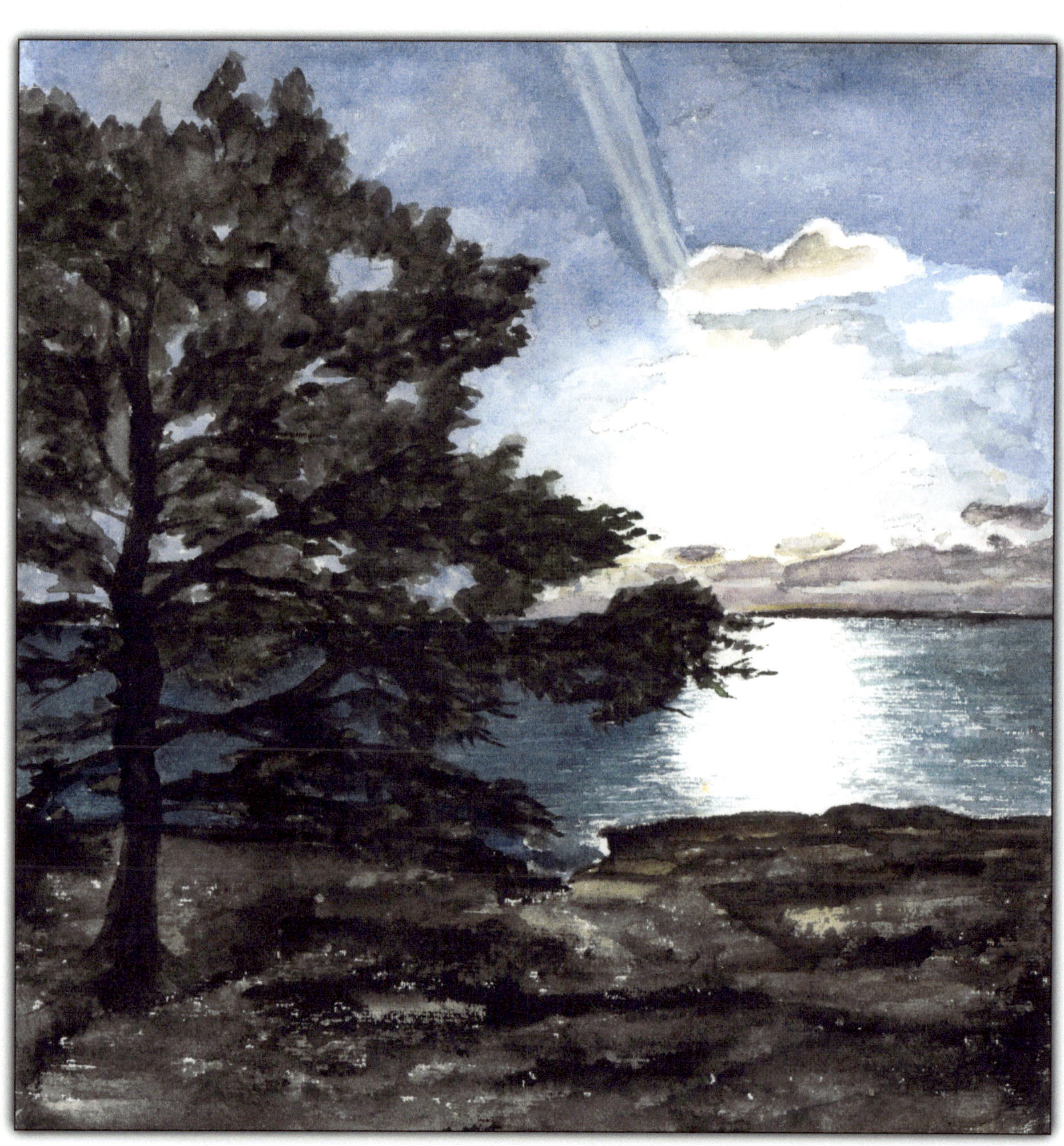

8 Or who shut up the sea with doors,
when it broke out of the womb,
9 when I made clouds its garment,
and wrapped it in thick darkness,
10 marked out for it my bound,
set bars and doors,
11 and said, 'You may come here, but no further.
Your proud waves shall be stopped here'?

Job 38:8-11

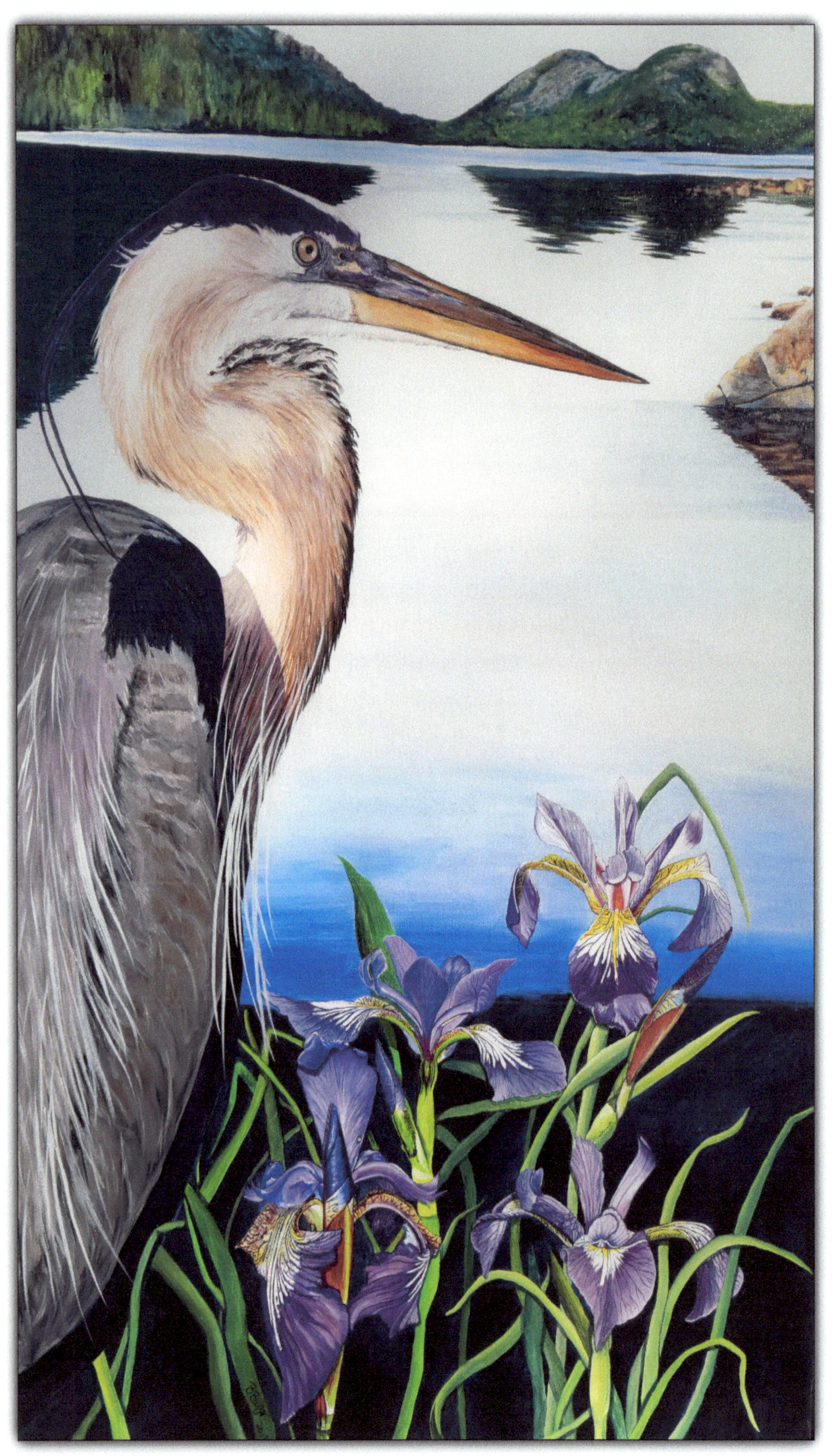

12 Have you commanded the morning in your days,
and caused the dawn to know its place,
13 that it might take hold of the ends of the earth,
and shake the wicked out of it?
14 It is changed as clay under the seal,
and presented as a garment.
15 From the wicked, their light is withheld.
The high arm is broken.

16 Have you entered into the springs of the sea?
Or have you walked in the recesses of the deep?

Job 38:12-16

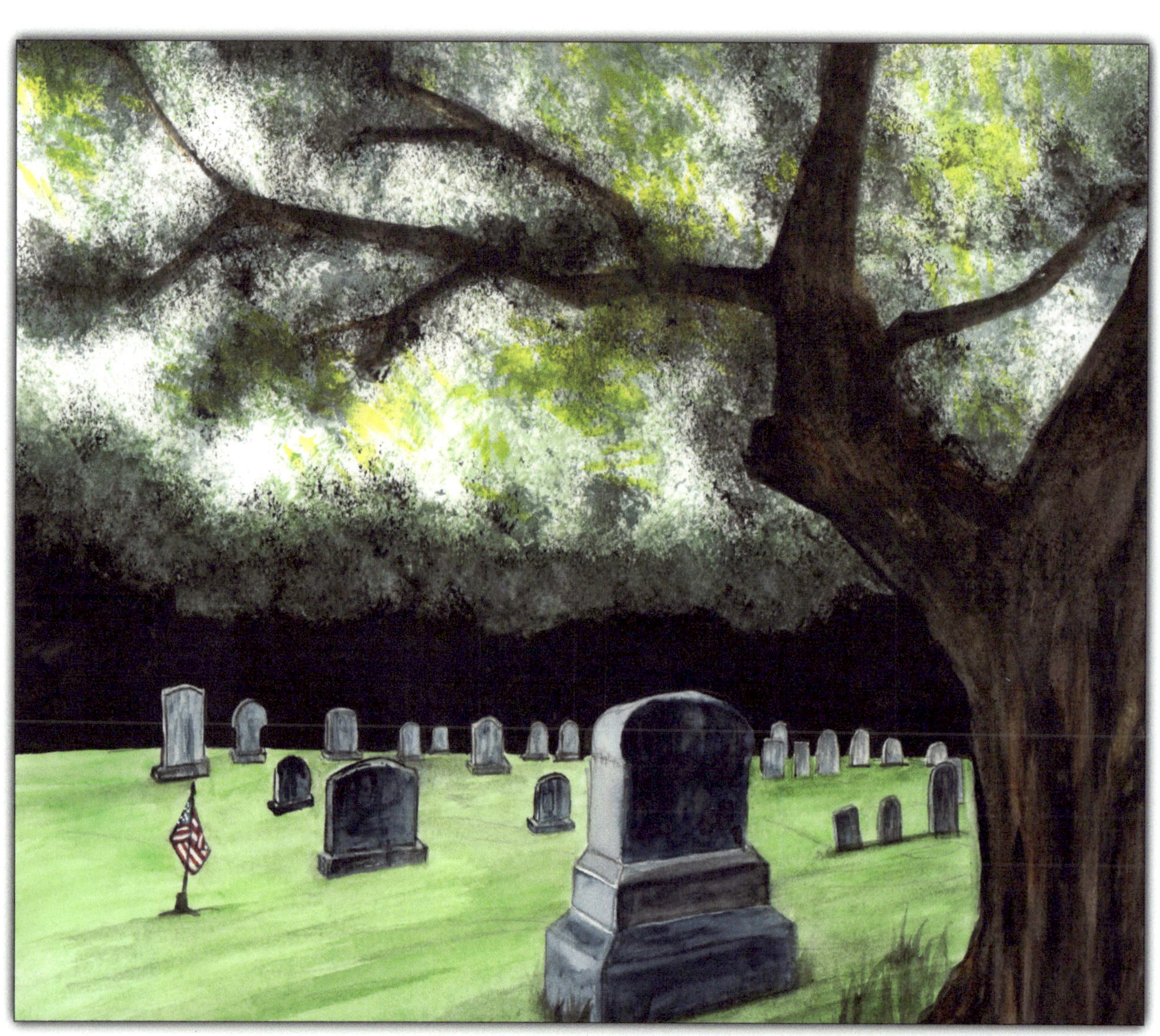

*17 Have the gates of death been revealed to you?
Or have you seen the gates of the shadow of death?*

Job 38:17

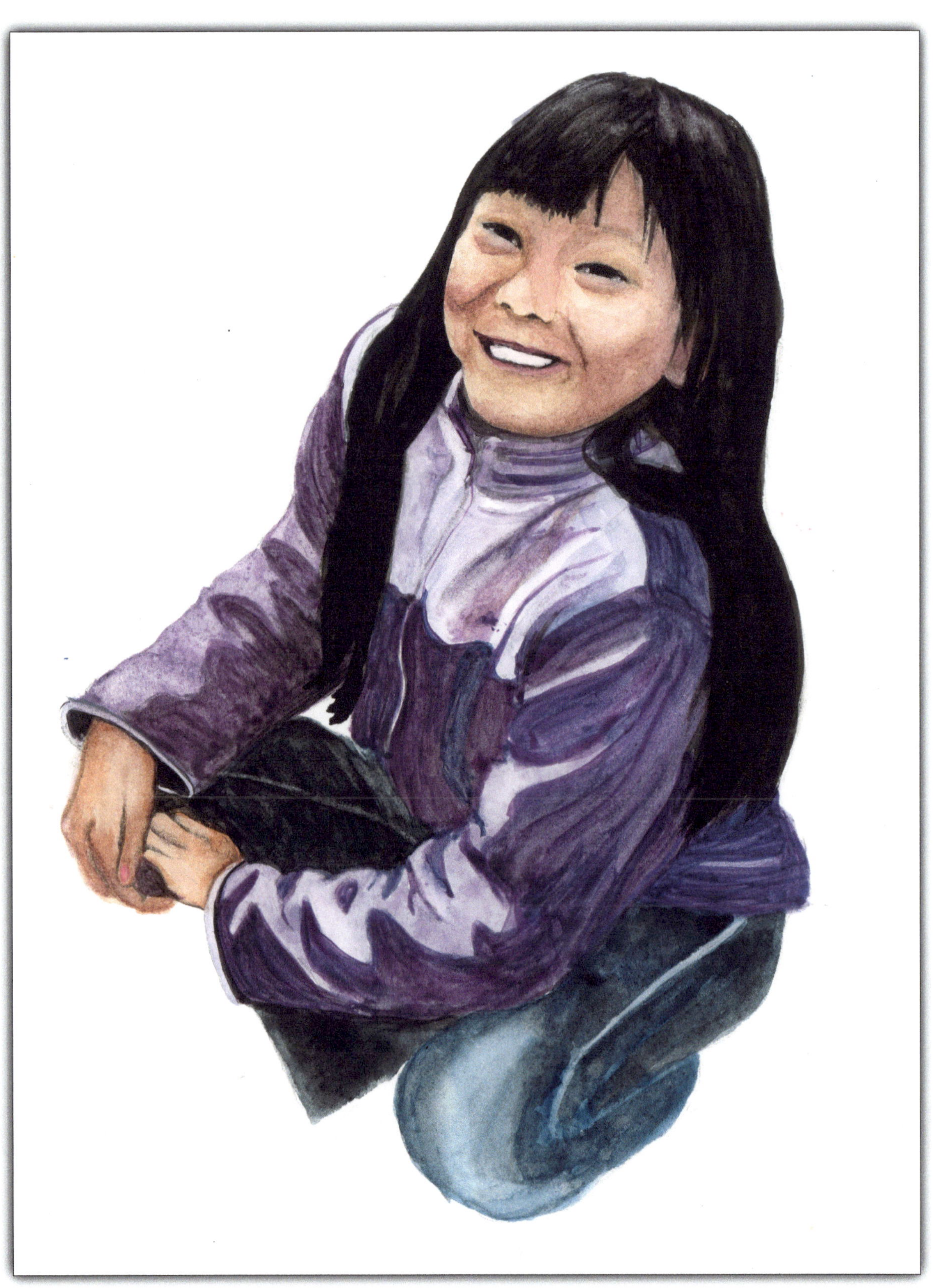

18 Have you comprehended the earth in its width?
Declare, if you know it all.

Job 38:18

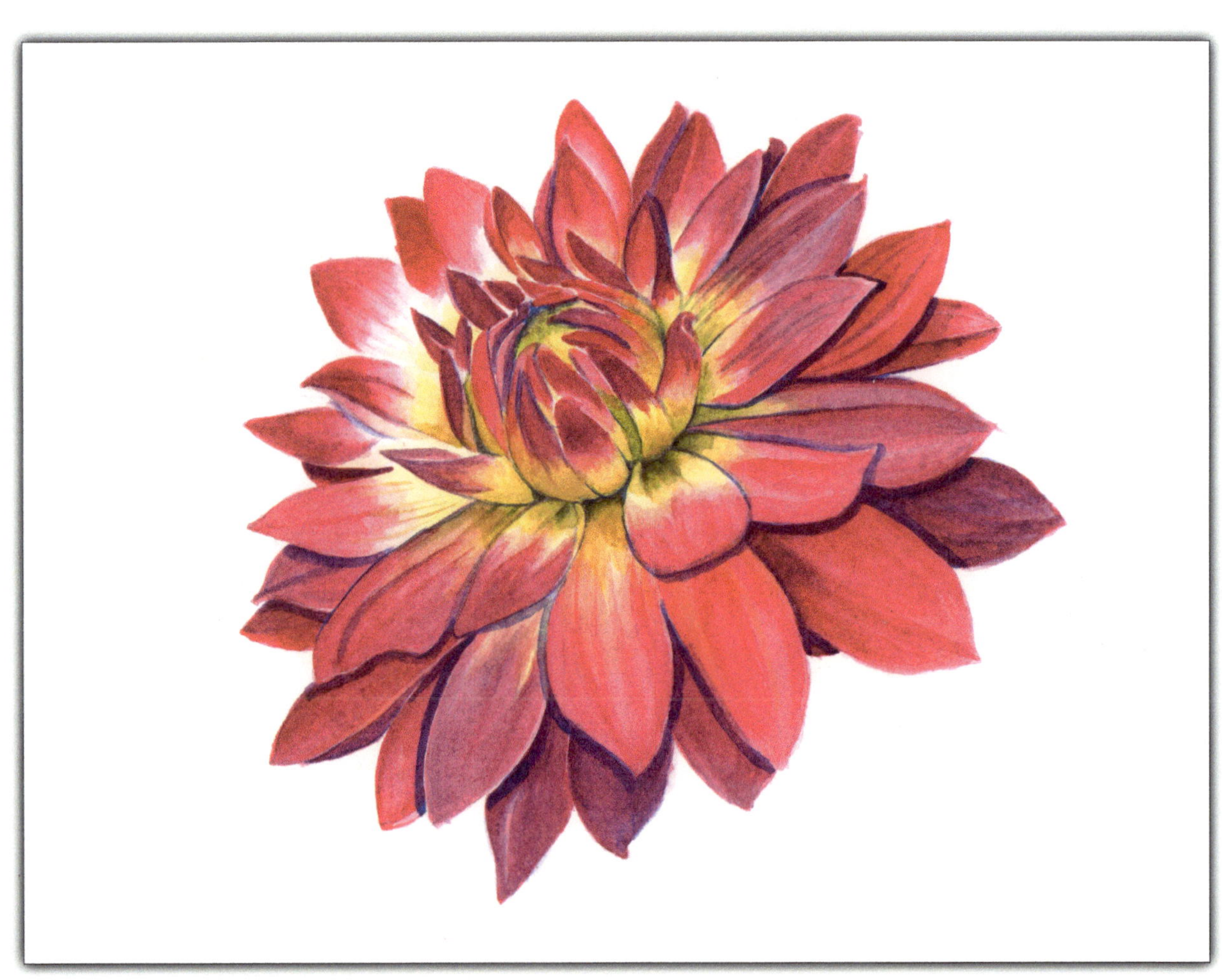

19 What is the way to the dwelling of light?
As for darkness, where is its place,
20 that you should take it to its bound,
that you should discern the paths to its house?
21 Surely you know, for you were born then,
and the number of your days is great!

Job 38:19-21

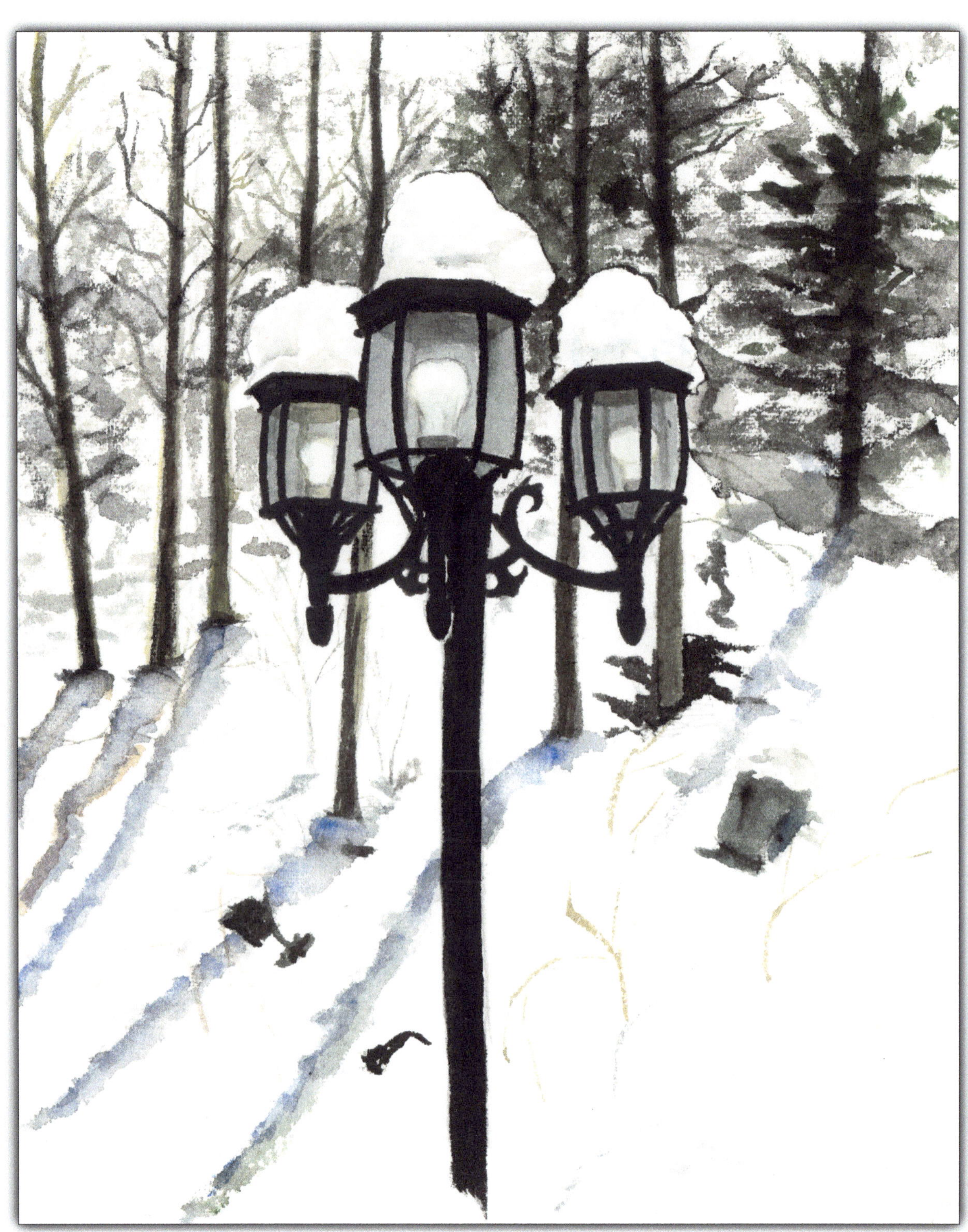

*22 Have you entered the storehouses of the snow,
or have you seen the storehouses of the hail,
23 which I have reserved against the time of trouble,
against the day of battle and war?*

Job 38:22-23

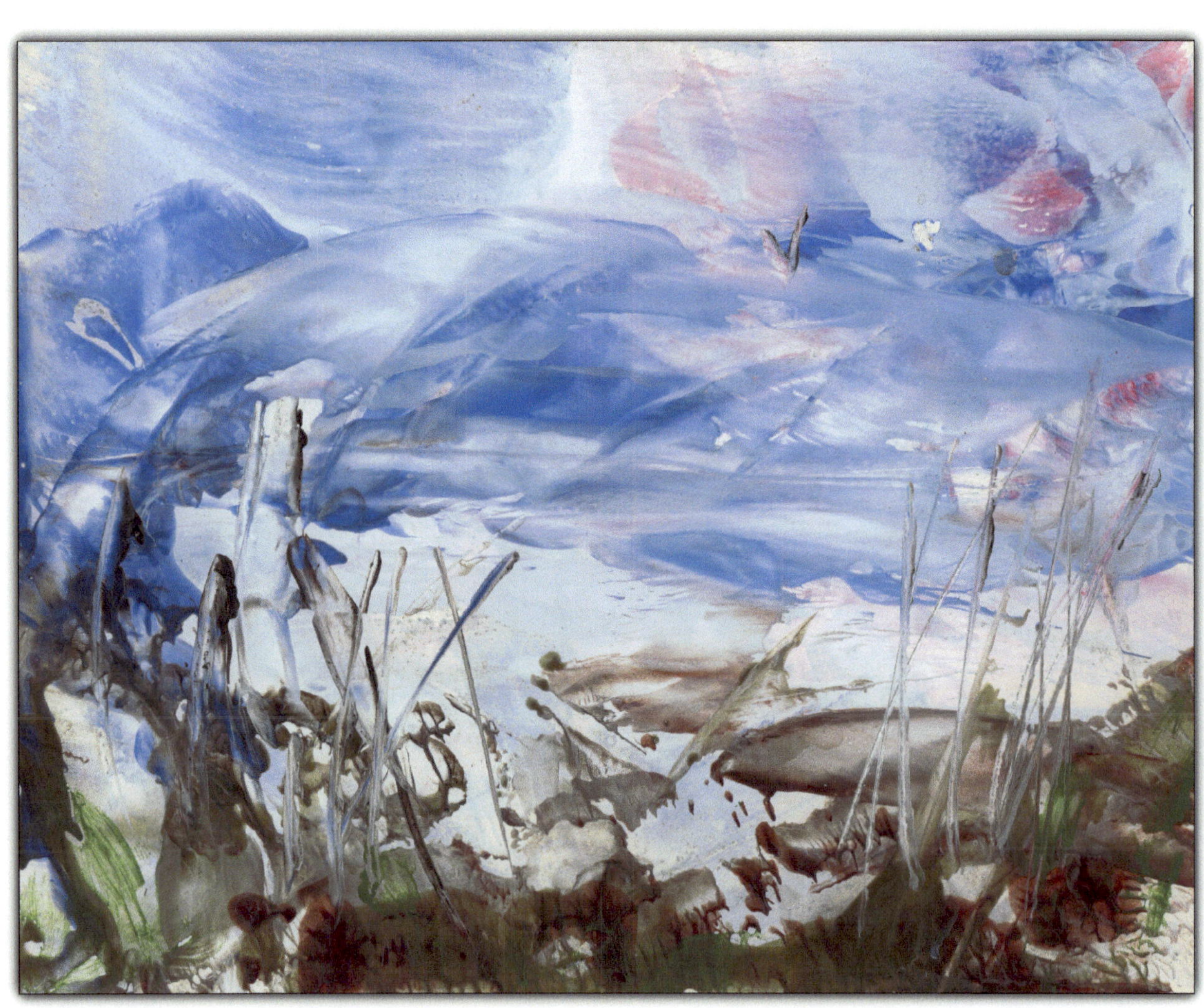

*24 By what way is the lightning distributed,
or the east wind scattered on the earth?*

Job 38:24

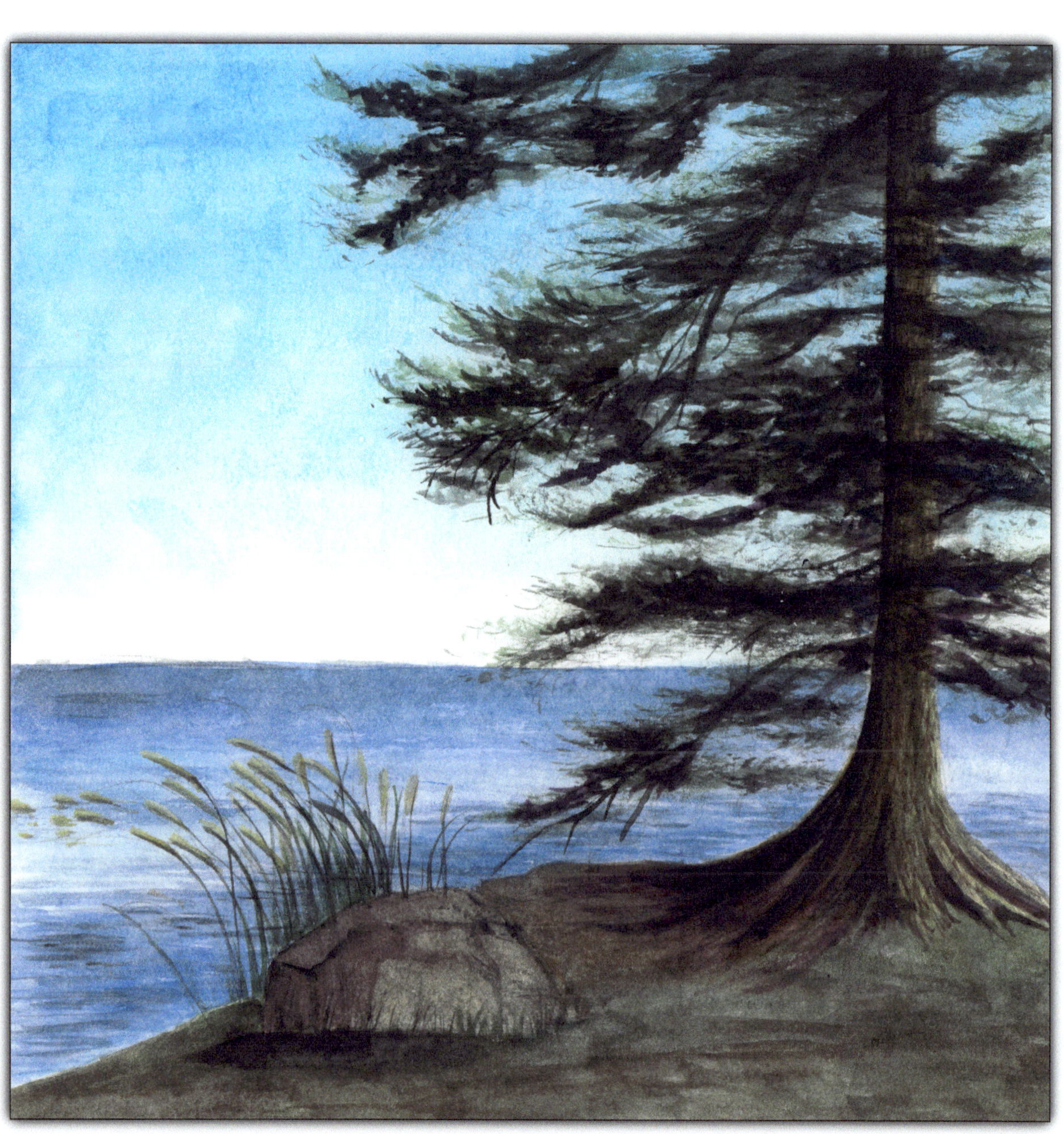

25 Who has cut a channel for the flood water,
or the path for the thunderstorm,
26 to cause it to rain on a land where there is no man,
on the wilderness, in which there is no man,
27 to satisfy the waste and desolate ground,
to cause the tender grass to grow?
28 Does the rain have a father?
Or who fathers the drops of dew?

Job 38:25-28

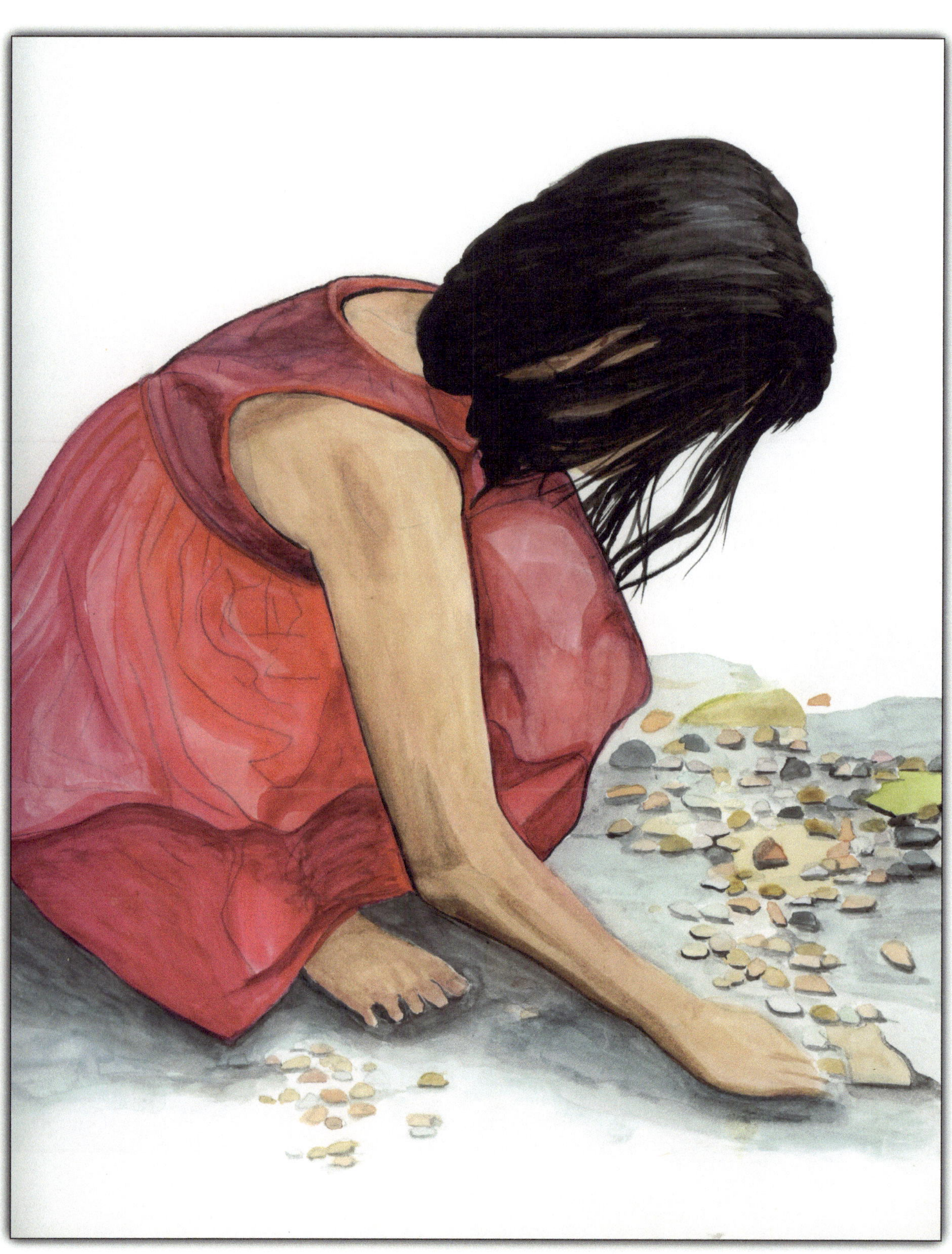

29 Whose womb did the ice come out of?
Who has given birth to the gray frost of the sky?
30 The waters become hard like stone,
when the surface of the deep is frozen.

Job 38: 29-30

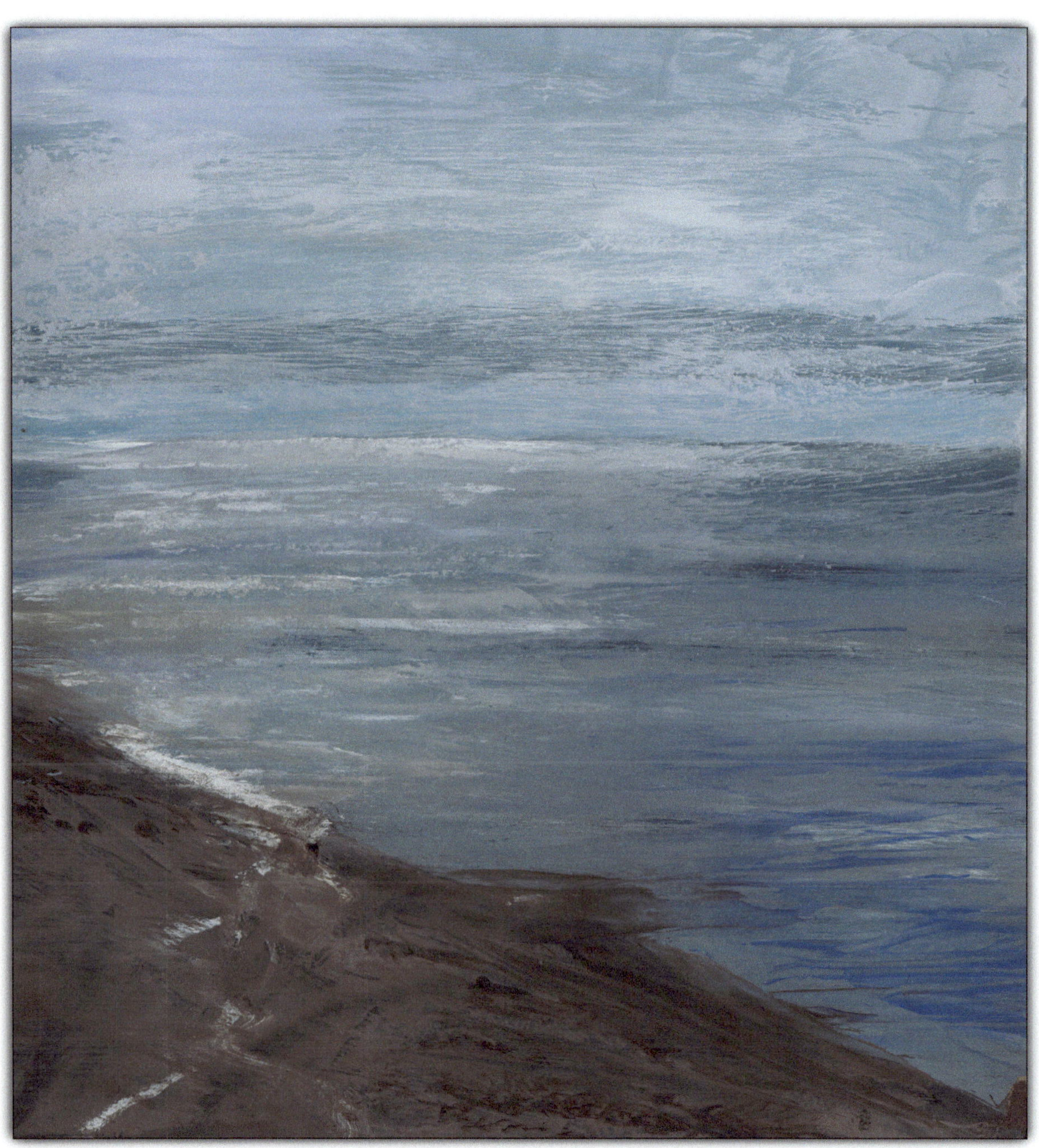

*31 Can you bind the cluster of the Pleiades,
or loosen the cords of Orion?
32 Can you lead the constellations out in their season?
Or can you guide the Bear with her cubs?*

Job 38: 31-32

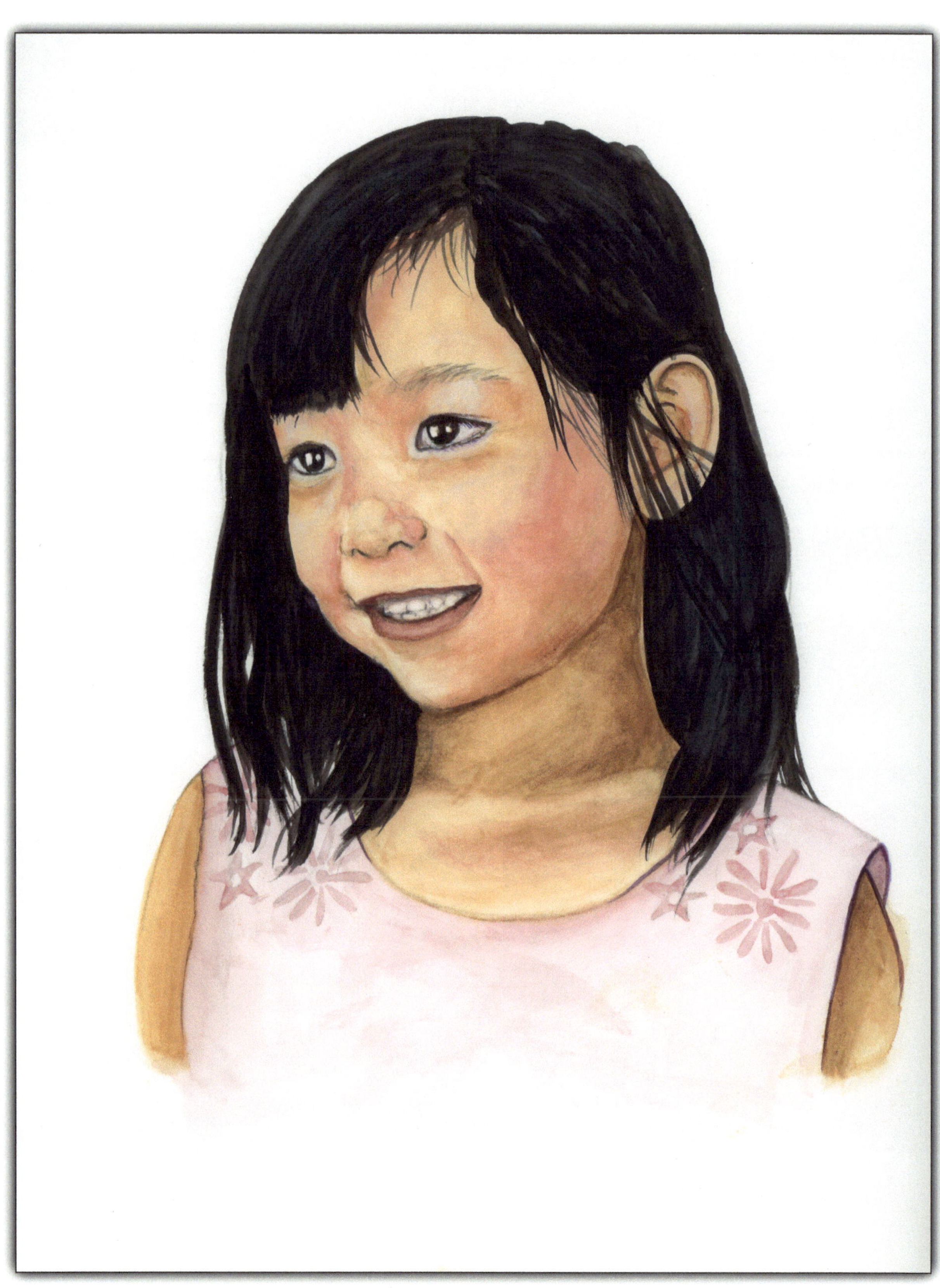

33 Do you know the laws of the heavens?
Can you establish its dominion over the earth?

Job 38:33

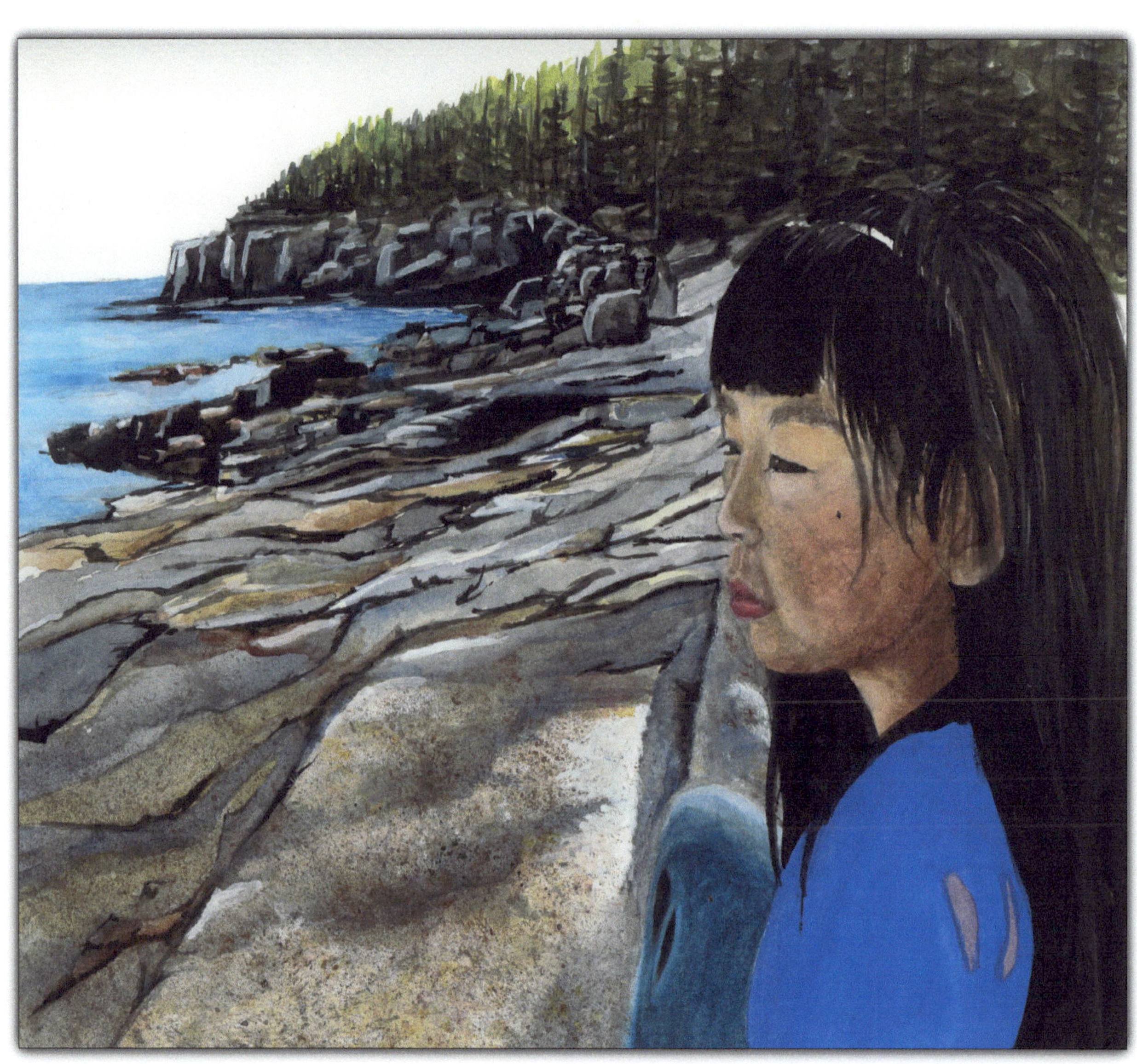

*34 Can you lift up your voice to the clouds,
that abundance of waters may cover you?
35 Can you send out lightnings, that they may go?
Do they report to you, 'Here we are'?*

Job 38:34-35

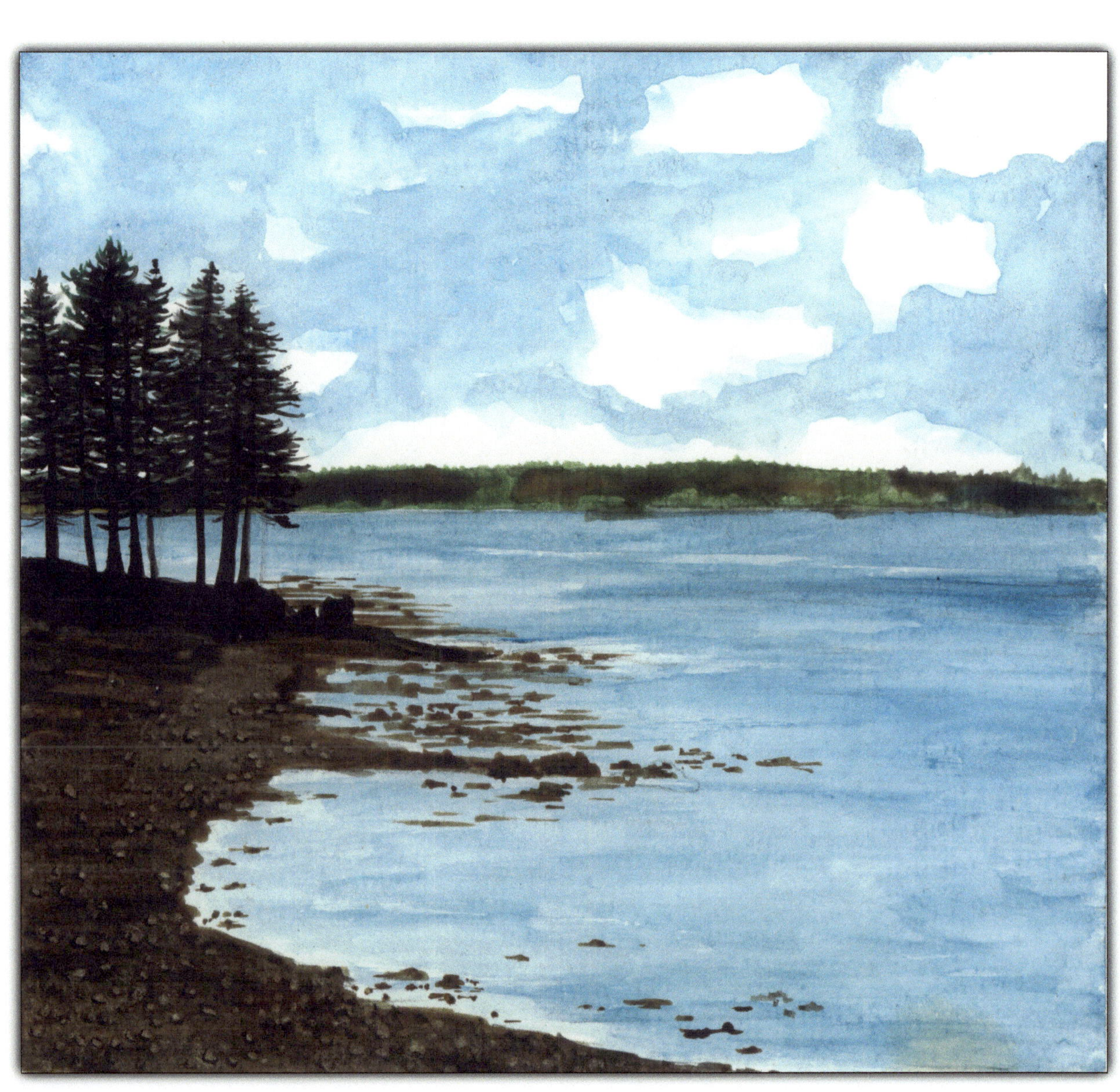

*36 Who has put wisdom in the inward parts?
Or who has given understanding to the mind?
37 Who can count the clouds by wisdom?
Or who can pour out the containers of the sky,*

Job 38:36-37

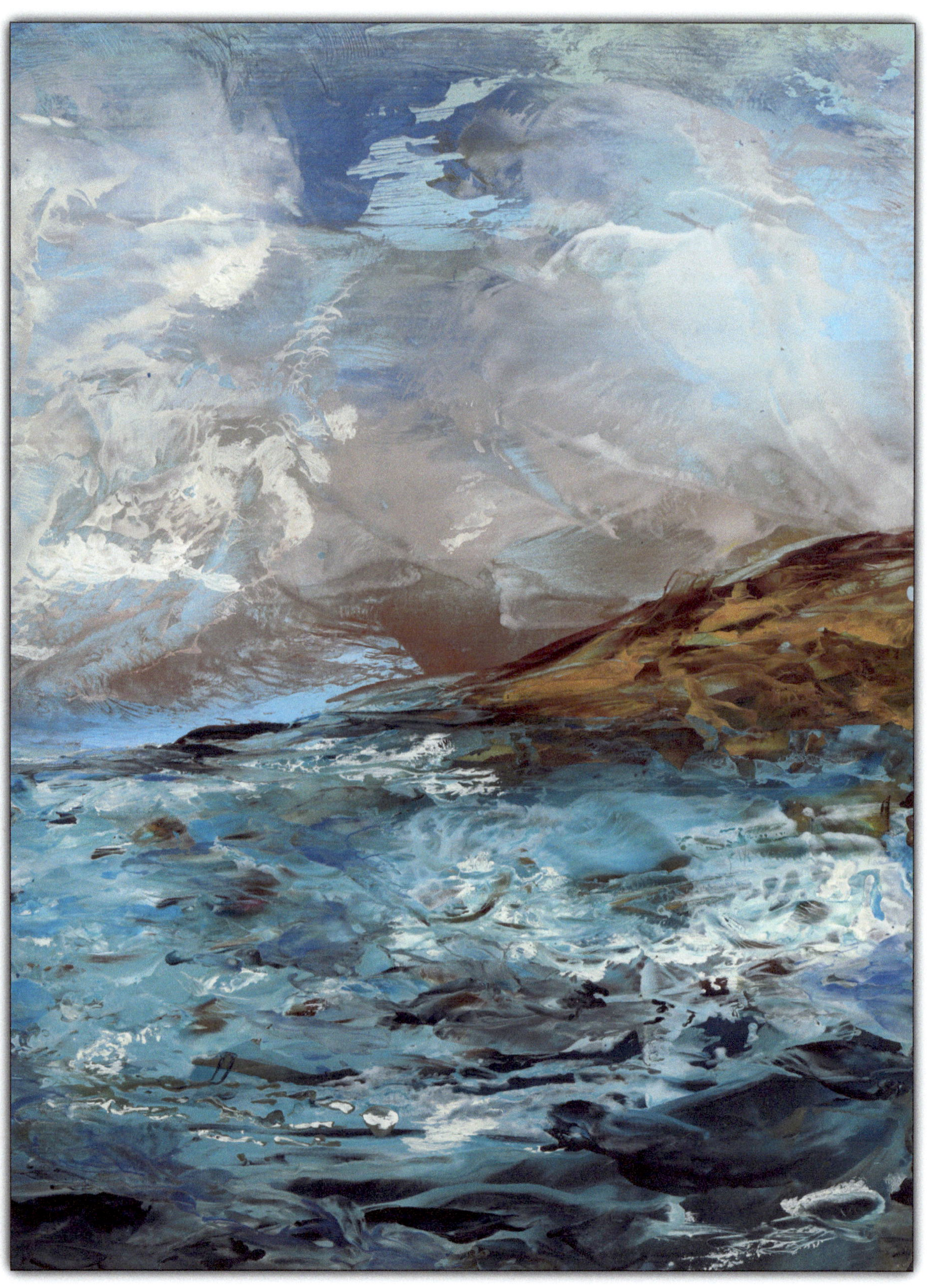

38 when the dust runs into a mass,
and the clods of earth stick together?

Job 38:38

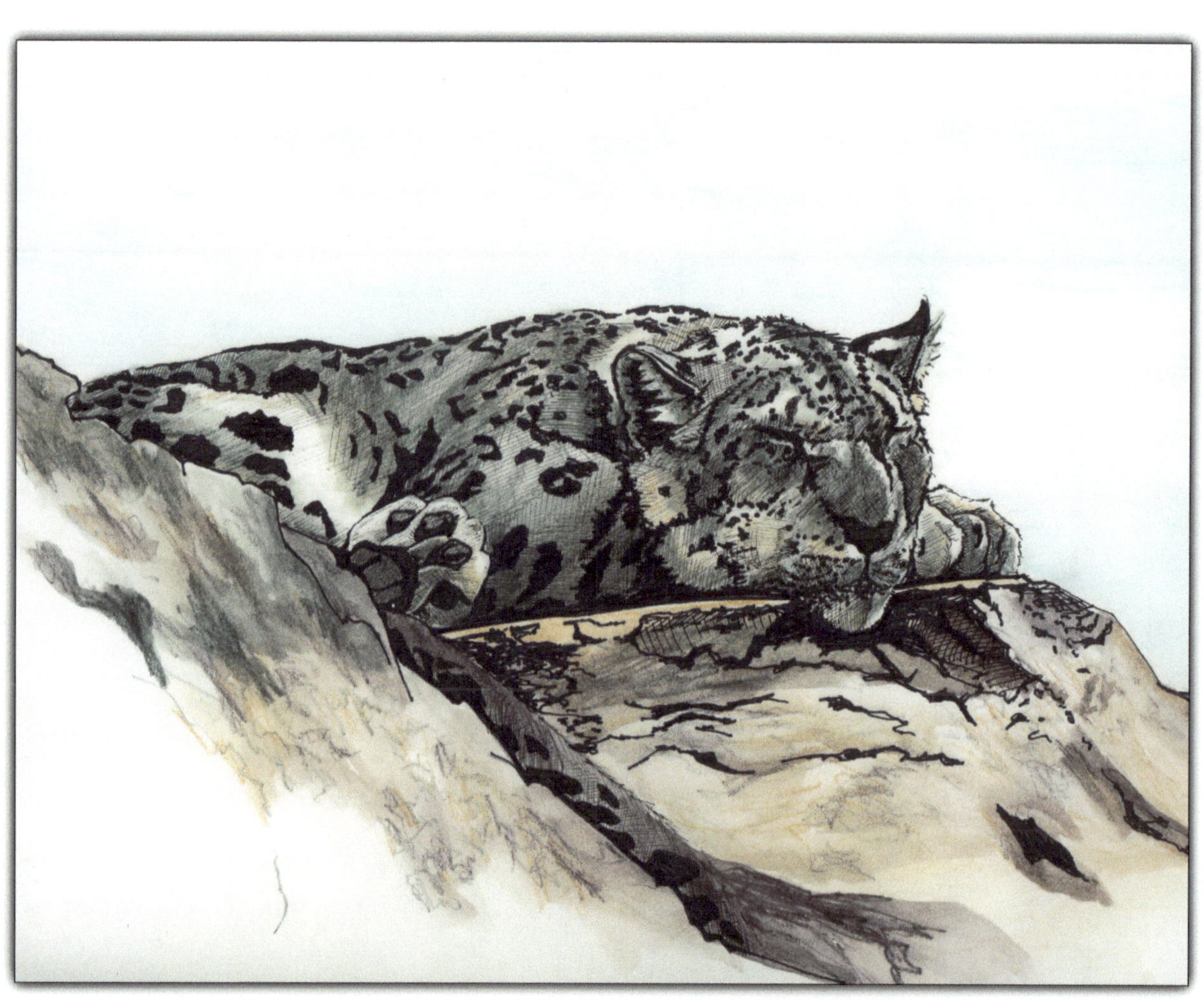

*39 Can you hunt the prey for the lioness,
or satisfy the appetite of the young lions,
40 when they crouch in their dens,
and lie in wait in the thicket?*

***Job 38:39-40*

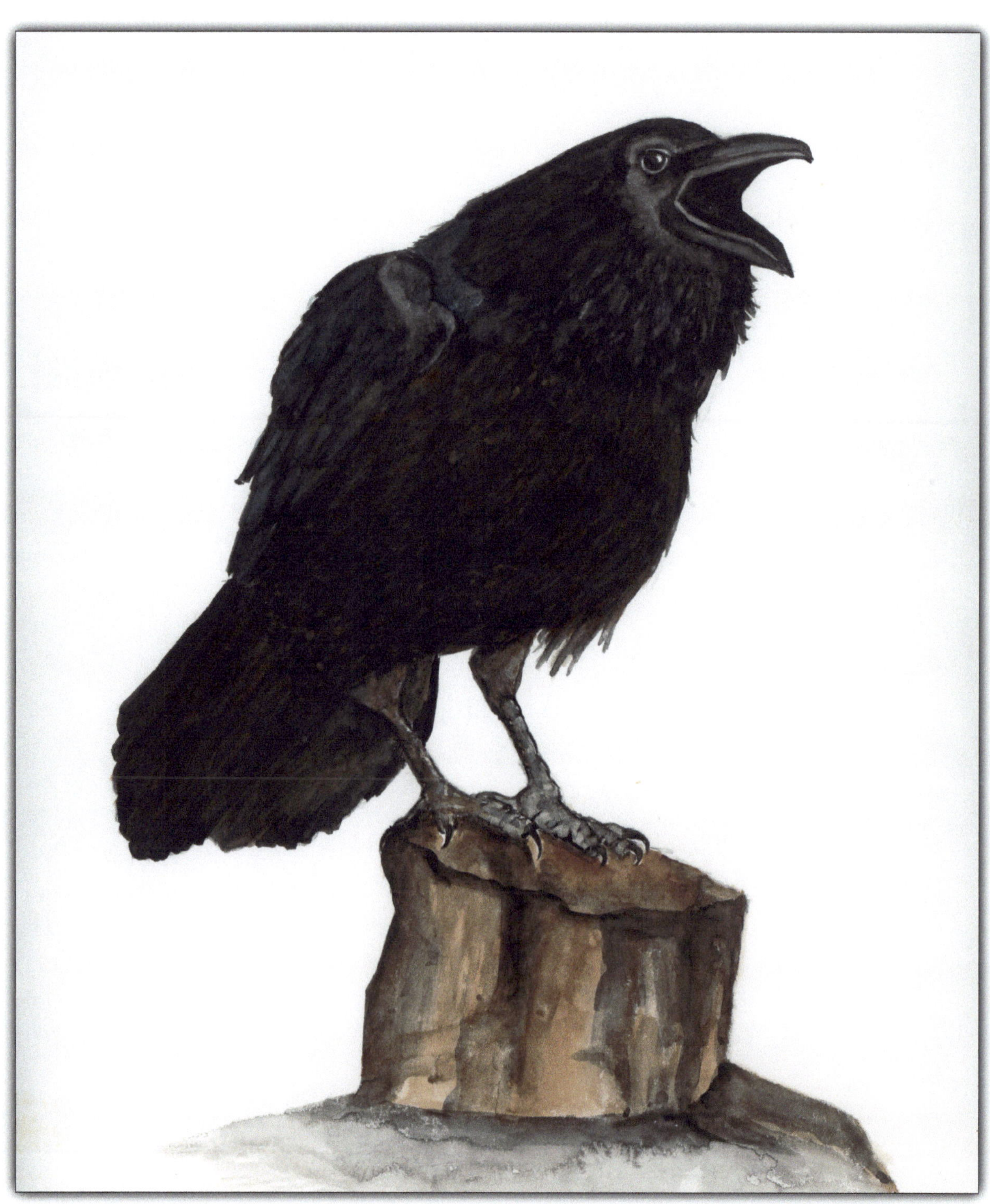

*41 Who provides for the raven his prey,
when his young ones cry to God,
and wander for lack of food?*

Job 38:41

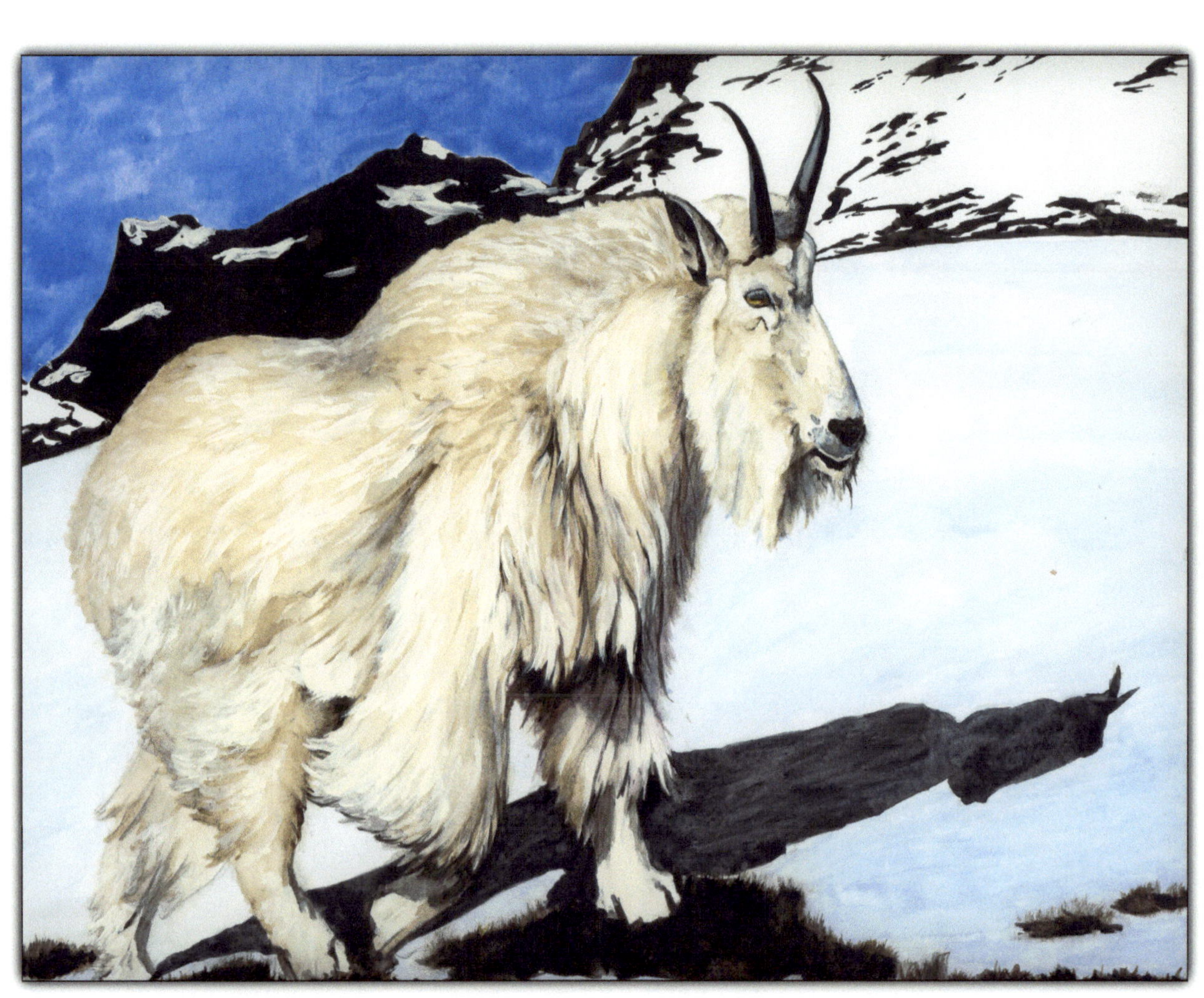

1 Do you know the time when the mountain goats give birth?
Do you watch when the doe bears fawns?
2 Can you count the months that they fulfill?
Or do you know the time when they give birth?

Job 39:1-2

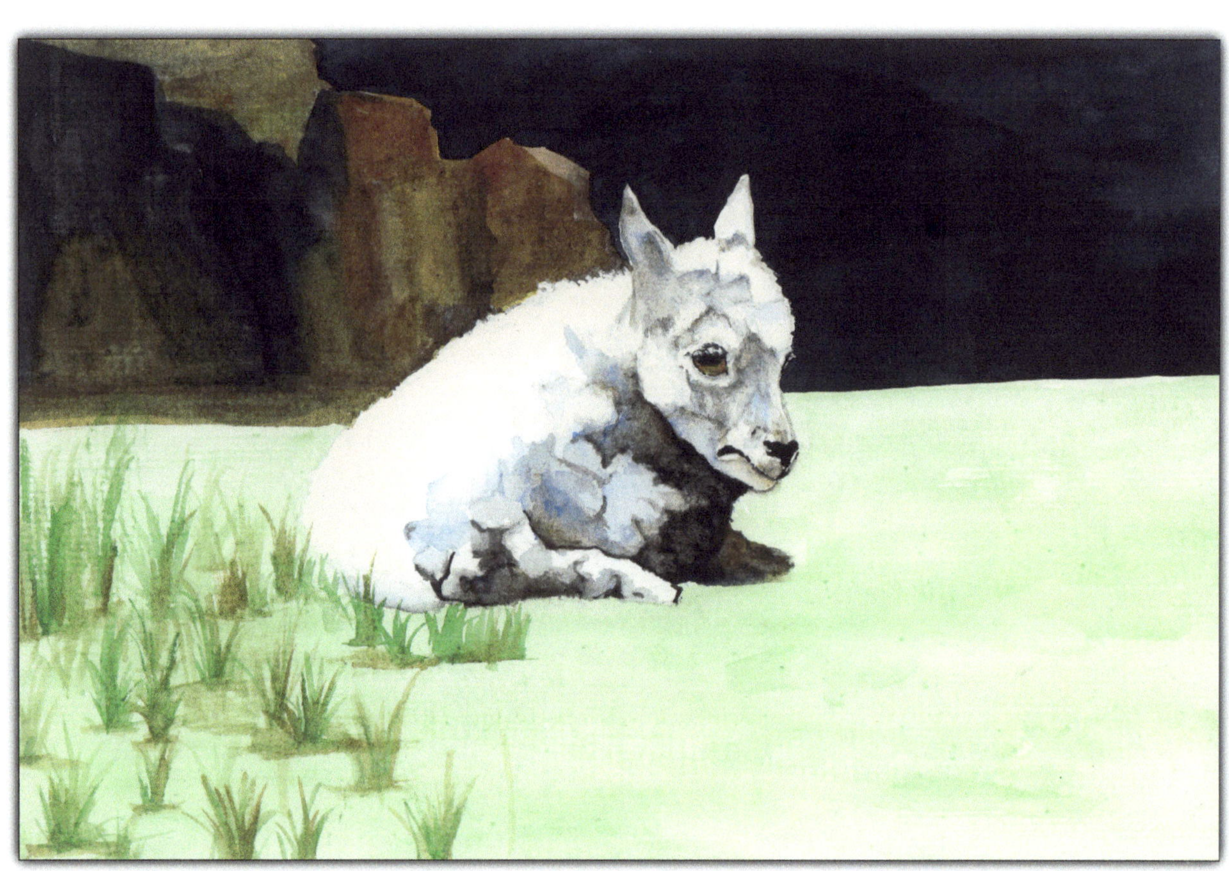

3 They bow themselves. They bear their young.
They end their labor pains.
4 Their young ones become strong.
They grow up in the open field.
They go out, and don't return again.

Job 39:3-4

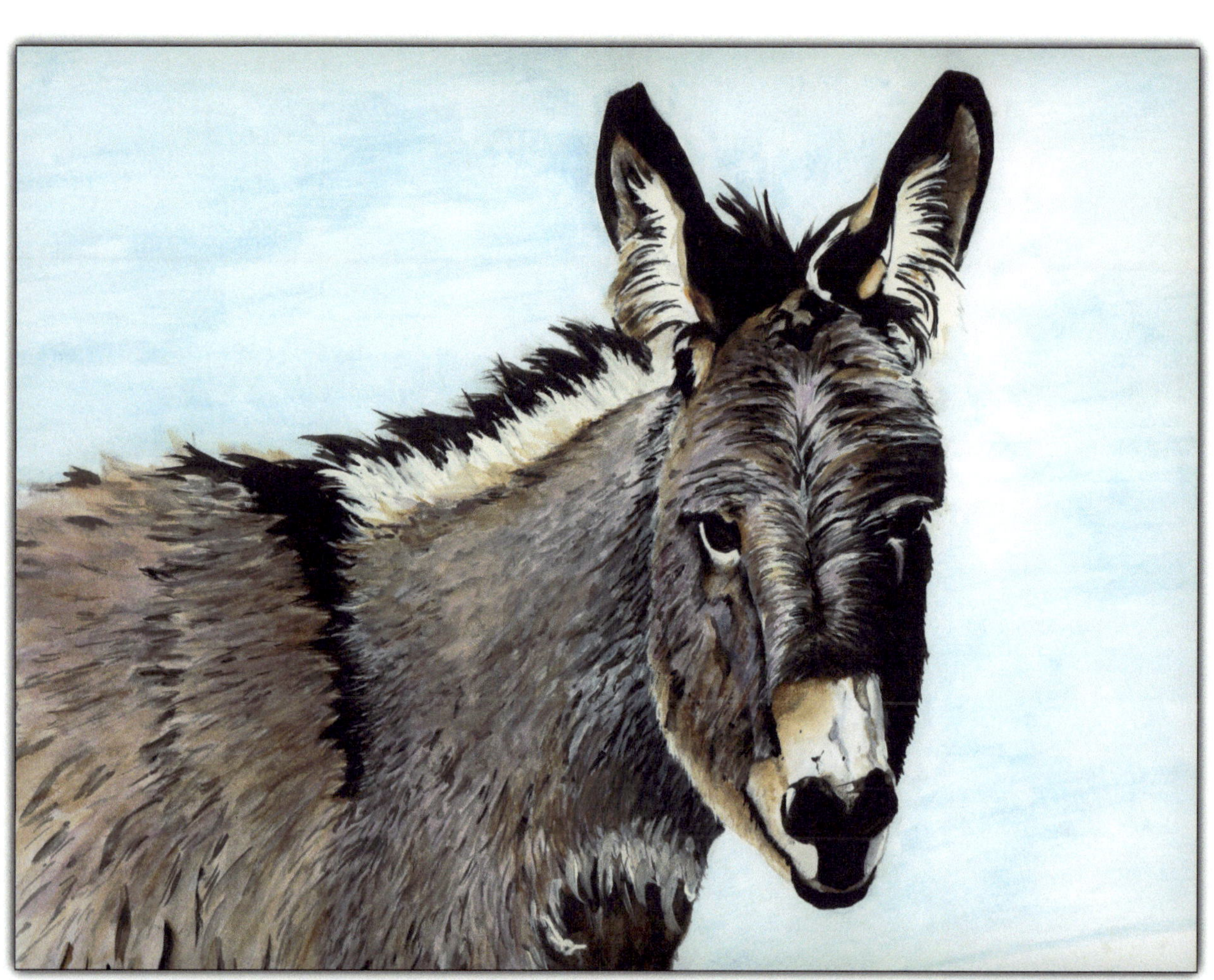

5 Who has set the wild donkey free?
Or who has loosened the bonds of the swift donkey,
6 whose home I have made the wilderness,
and the salt land his dwelling place?
7 He scorns the tumult of the city,
neither does he hear the shouting of the driver.
8 The range of the mountains is his pasture.
He searches after every green thing.

Job 39:5-8

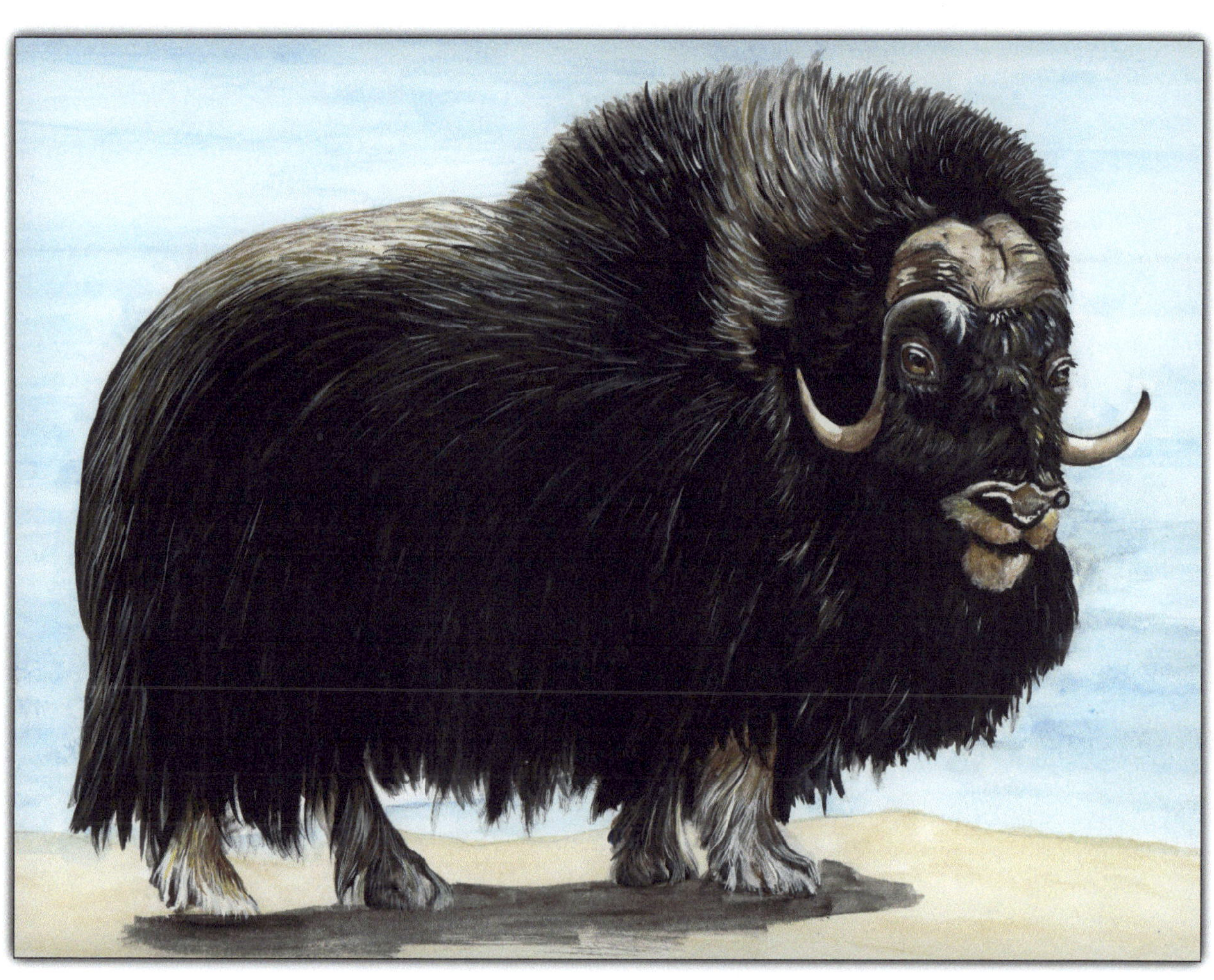

9 Will the wild ox be content to serve you?
Or will he stay by your feeding trough?
10 Can you hold the wild ox in the furrow with his harness?
Or will he till the valleys after you?
11 Will you trust him, because his strength is great?
Or will you leave to him your labor?
12 Will you confide in him, that he will bring home your seed,
and gather the grain of your threshing floor?

Job 39:9-12

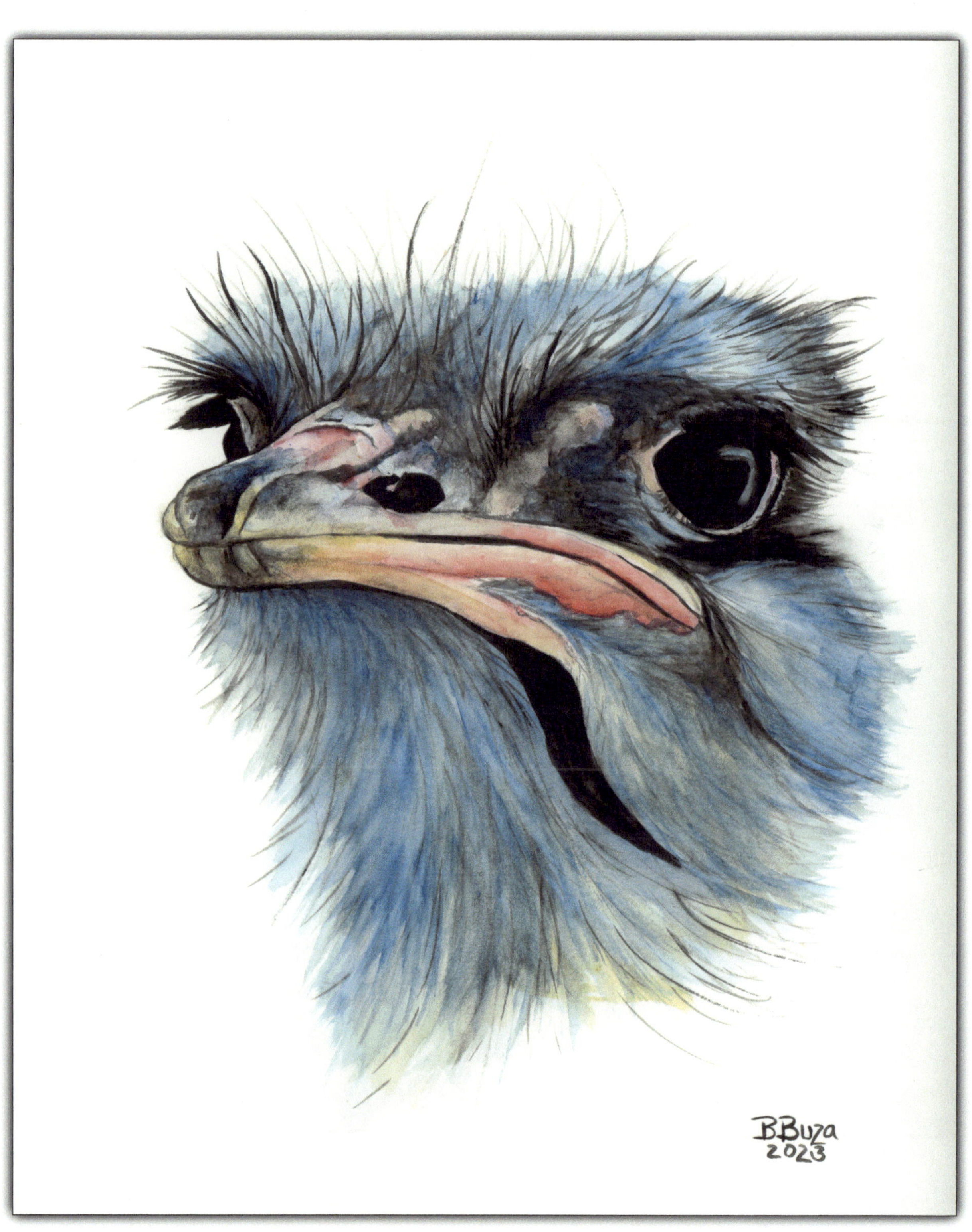
B.Buza
2023

*13 The wings of the ostrich wave proudly,
but are they the feathers and plumage of love?*

Job 39:13

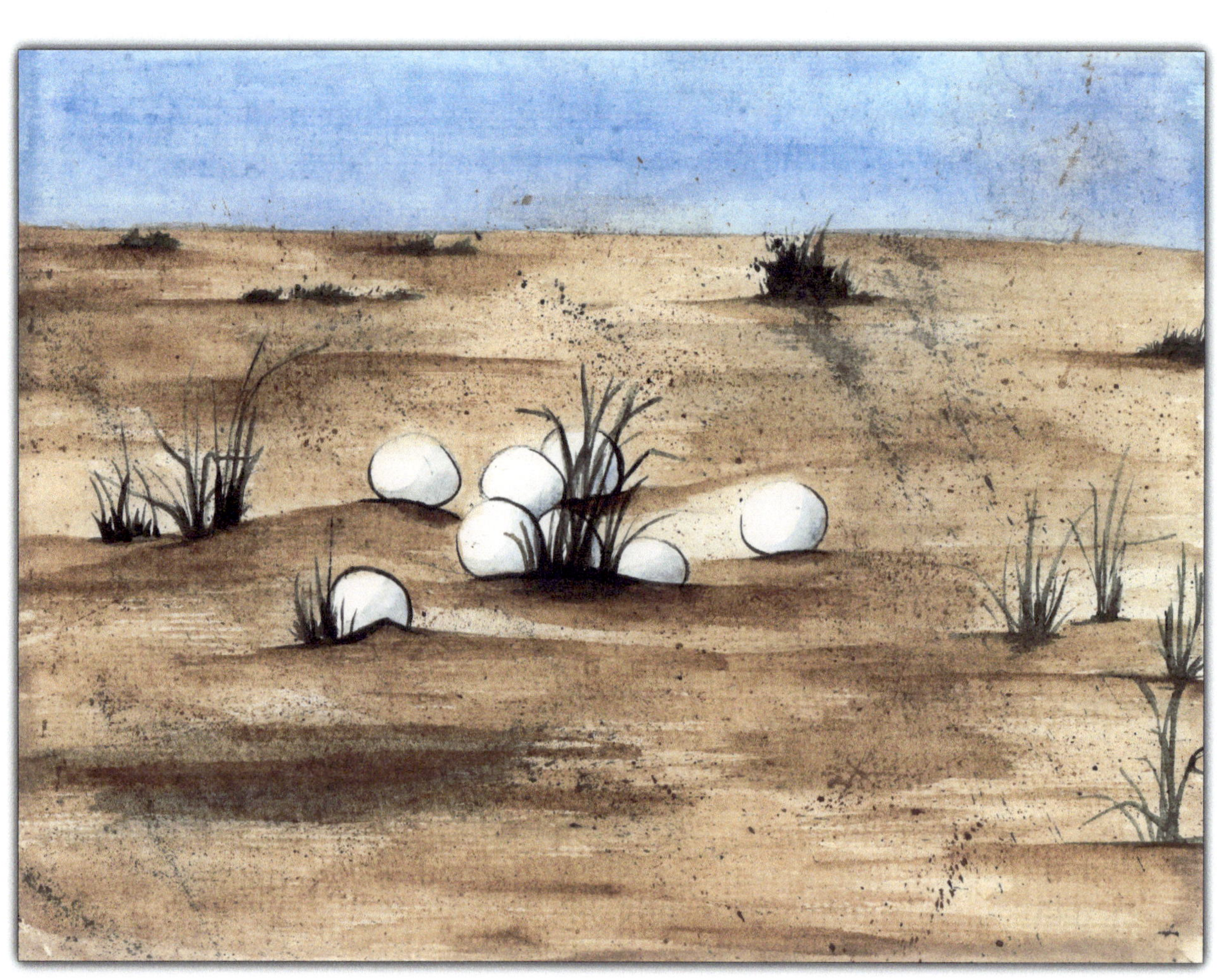

14 For she leaves her eggs on the earth,
warms them in the dust,
15 and forgets that the foot may crush them,
or that the wild animal may trample them.
16 She deals harshly with her young ones, as if they were not hers.
Though her labor is in vain, she is without fear,
17 because God has deprived her of wisdom,
neither has he imparted to her understanding.
18 When she lifts up herself on high,
she scorns the horse and his rider.

Job 39:14-18

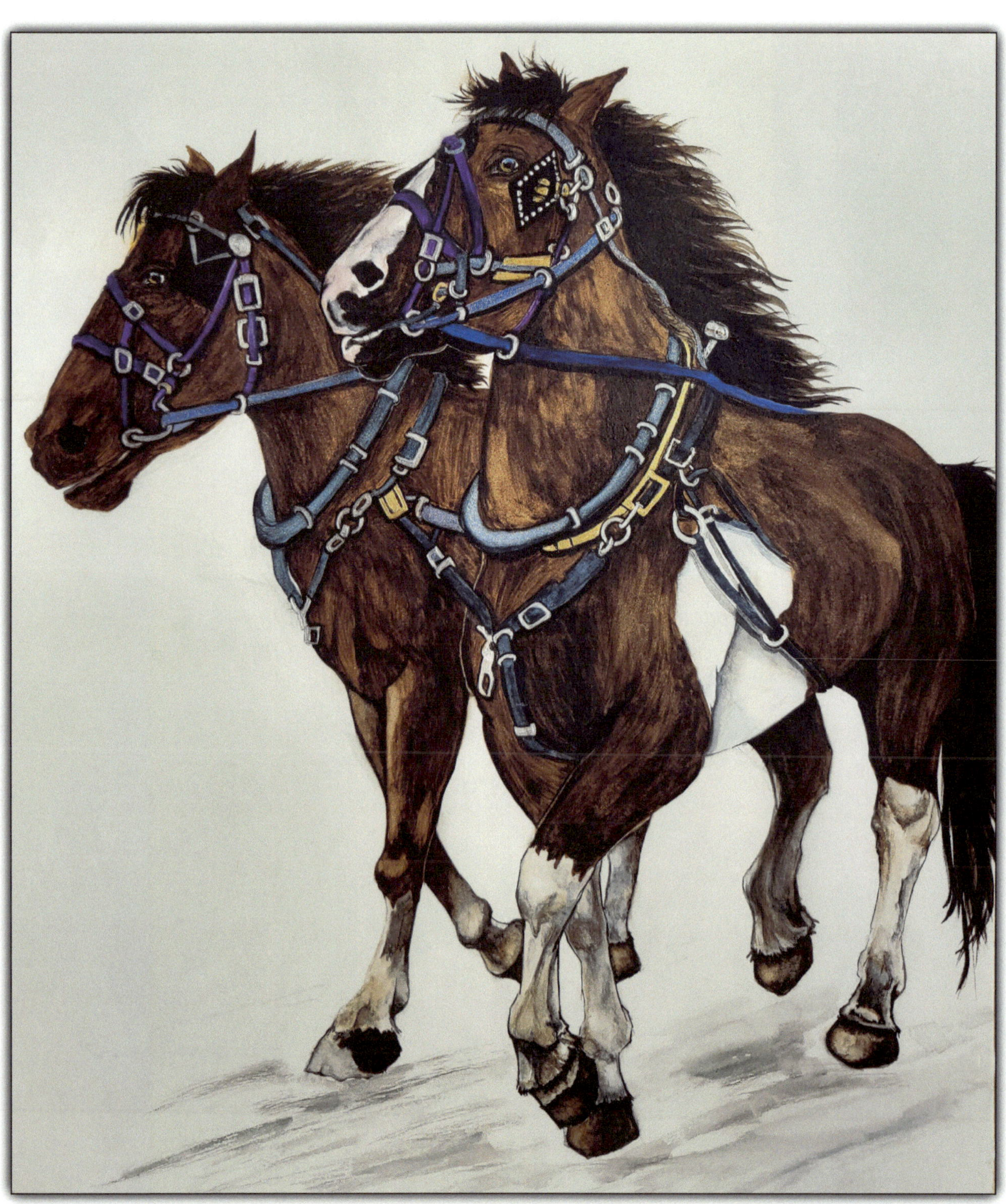

19 Have you given the horse might?
Have you clothed his neck with a quivering mane?
20 Have you made him to leap as a locust?
The glory of his snorting is awesome.
21 He paws in the valley, and rejoices in his strength.
He goes out to meet the armed men.
22 He mocks at fear, and is not dismayed,
neither does he turn back from the sword.
23 The quiver rattles against him,
the flashing spear and the javelin.
24 He eats up the ground with fierceness and rage,
neither does he stand still at the sound of the trumpet.
25 As often as the trumpet sounds he snorts, 'Aha!'
He smells the battle afar off,
the thunder of the captains, and the shouting.

Job 39:19-25

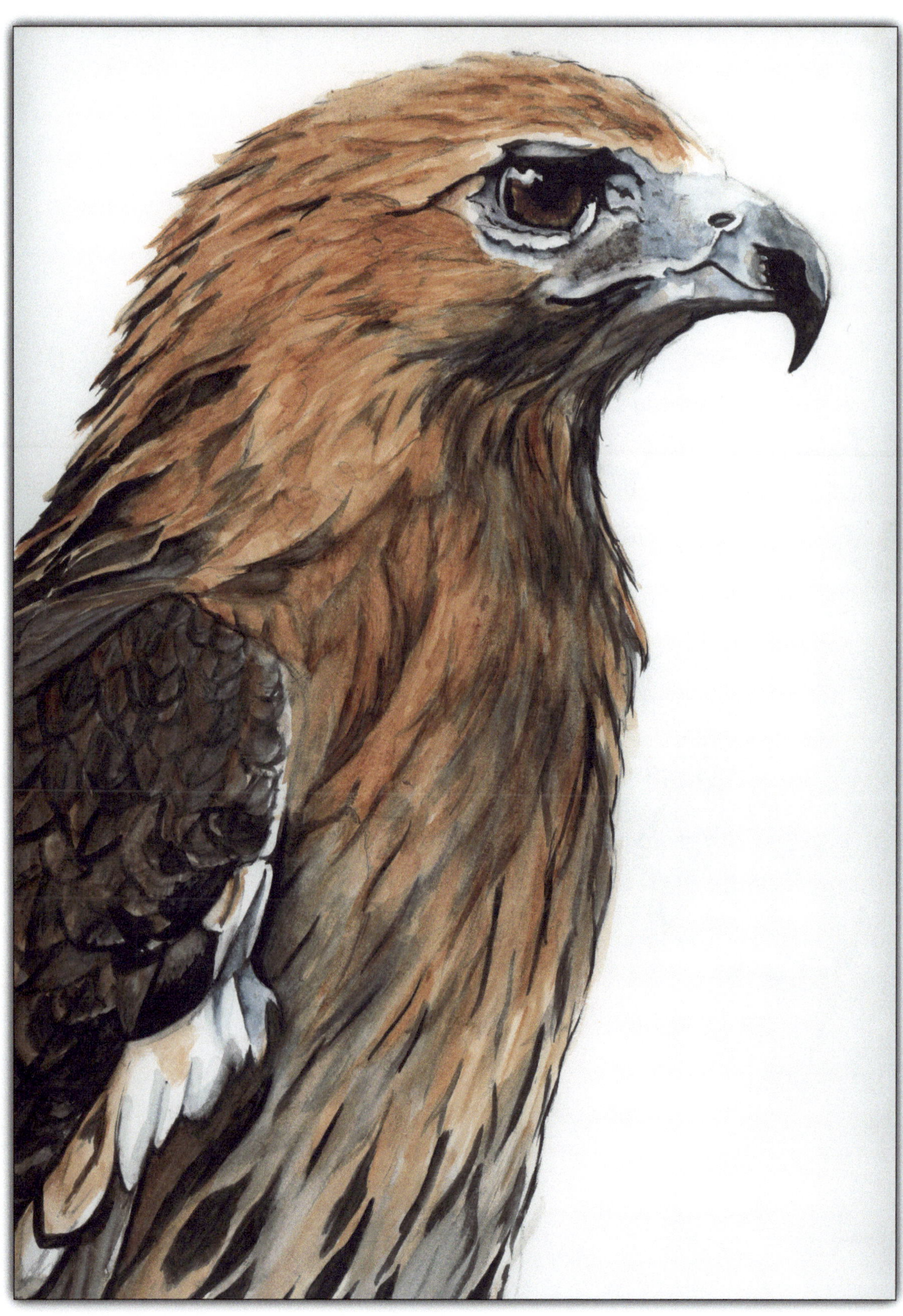

26 Is it by your wisdom that the hawk soars,
and stretches her wings toward the south?
27 Is it at your command that the eagle mounts up,
and makes his nest on high?
28 On the cliff he dwells and makes his home,
on the point of the cliff and the stronghold.
29 From there he spies out the prey.
His eyes see it afar off.
30 His young ones also suck up blood.
Where the slain are, there he is."

Job 39:26-30

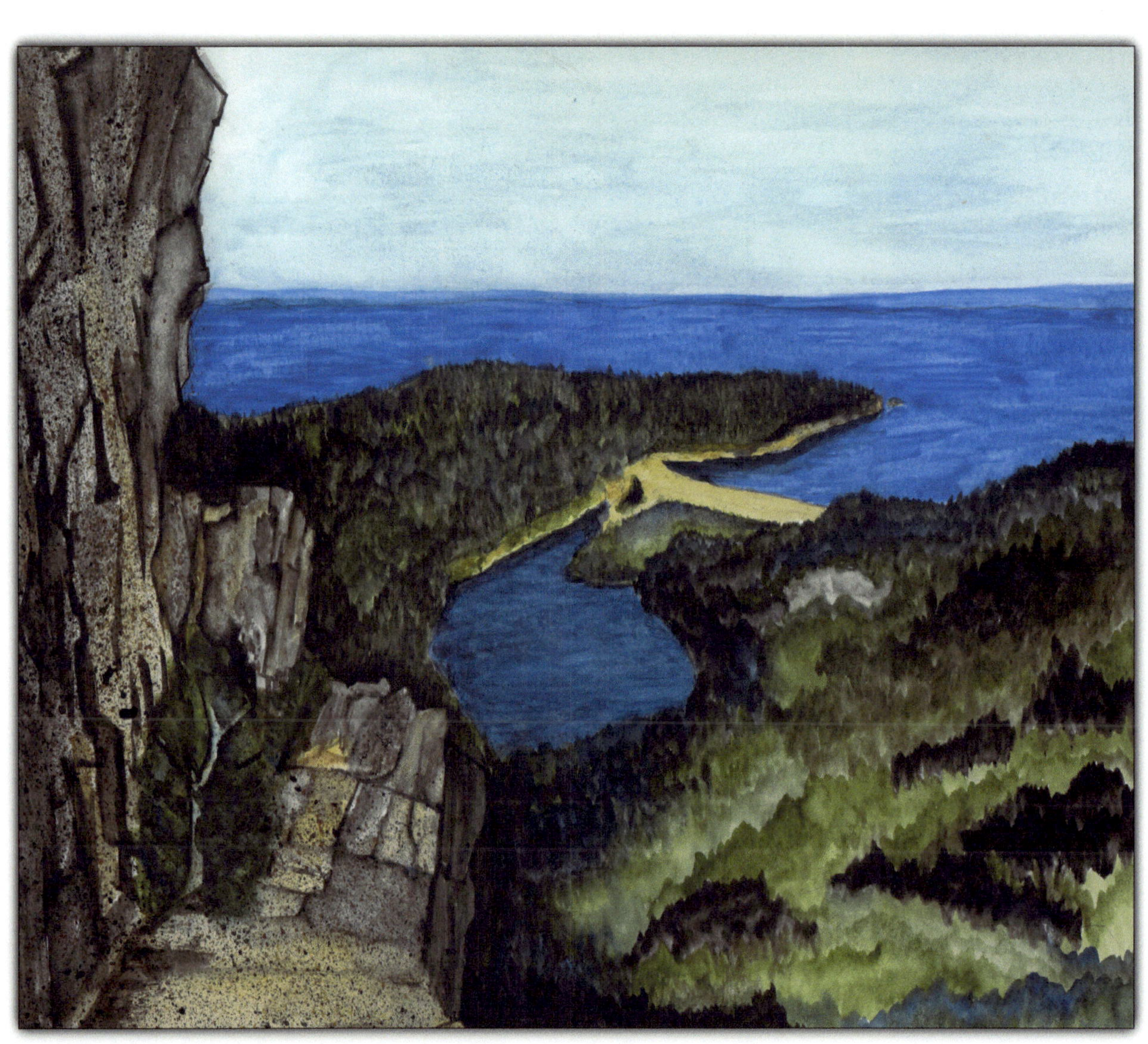

ABOUT THE ARTIST

Barb Buza is a self-taught artist who specializes in realism. She enjoys experimenting with a wide variety of subjects in her art, and has a special passion for silk painting and mixing mediums.

After living and working in New England as a nurse for three decades while raising her three daughters, she now splits her time between the rocky coasts of Maine and the rolling hills of Kentucky.

Now able to focus on God's calling for her life, she is working to present the stories and scriptures of the Bible through her God-given talent for art.

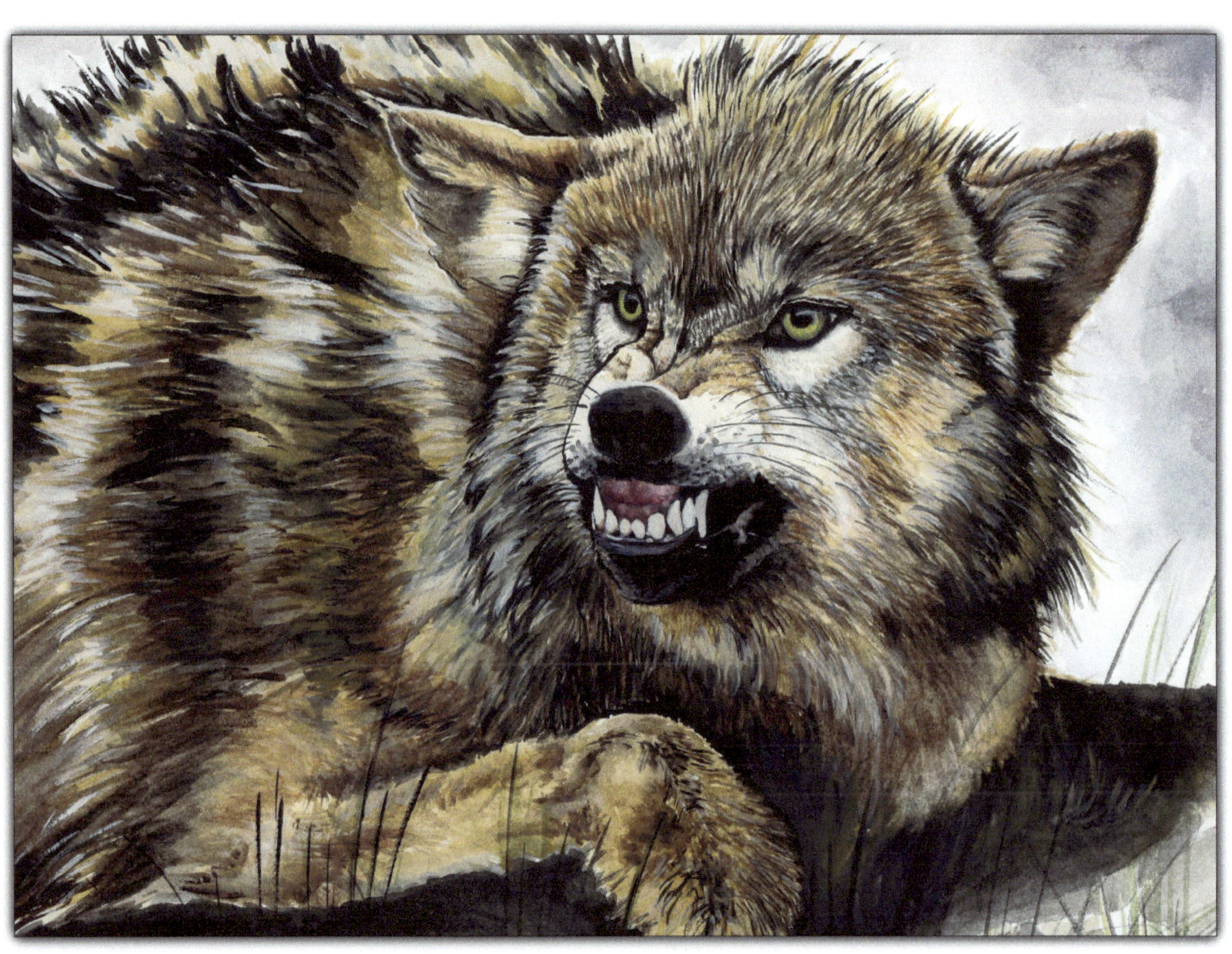